PINK FLOYD
REVEALED

Publisher and Creative Director: Nick Wells
Project Editor and Picture Research: Sara Robson
Art Director: Mike Spender
Layout Design: Theresa Maynard
Digital Design and Production: Chris Herbert

Special thanks to: Frances Bodiam, Chelsea Edwards, Cat Emslie, Rebecca Kidd, Victoria Lyle, Geoffrey Meadon, Polly Prior, Sam Shore and Helen Tovey

Ian Shirley (author) lived and pogoed his way through British punk rock and has been buying records and watching bands ever since. He is an experienced music journalist whose feature work and reviews appear in respected magazines like *Record Collector* and *Goldmine*. He has written the biographies of Bauhaus, and The Residents as well as two science-fiction novels. He has also written the definitive tome on the links between comics and music: *Can Rock And Roll Save The World*, and contributed to Flame Tree's *The Definitive Illustrated Encyclopedia of Rock*. He is currently the editor of *Record Collector*'s *Rare Record Price Guide* and has a collection of over 2,000 vinyl albums, 4,000 45rpm singles and 5,000 CDs.

Jerry Ewing (Foreword) is the editor of *Classic Rock Presents Prog* magazine. He set up *Classic Rock* magazine for Dennis Publishing in 1998 and prior to that was deputy editor of *Metal Hammer* magazine. He still writes for both *Classic Rock* and *Metal Hammer*, as well as *Maxim*, *Bizarre* and *Rocks* magazine in Germany. He has several books to his name on the likes of AC/DC, Led Zeppelin and Metallica and has a raft of appearances on TV and DVD, as well as doing voice-over work. He has also presented radio shows on *Total Rock* for 10 years.

Picture Credits
Alamy Images: Content Mine International: 114, 194 (t); INTERFOTO Pressebildagentur: 14; Pictorial Press Ltd: 17 (t), 33, 35, 50, 51, 59; Sarah Quill: 148; Vic Singh Studio: 31; Stu: 176; Trinity Mirror/Mirrorpix: 19, 23; Victor Watts: 128. **Corbis:** Alain Nogues/CORBIS SYGMA: 63; Denis O'Regan: 156–57, 161; Neal Preston: 106–07, 134–35, 153, 168 (t). **Foundry Arts:** 17 (b), 25 (b), 38 (r), 47, 49, 55 (t), 56 (r), 57, 58 (b), 66 (b), 67, 68 (r), 72, 74 (b), 76 (b), 77 (t), 79 (t), 86, 89 (b), 93 (l, r), 97, 99 (b), 109 (b), 110 (b), 113 (l), 116, 118 (l, r), 122 (c, r), 127, 129 (l), 136, 139, 140 (b), 144 (b), 147 (b), 149 (t), 152 (r), 155 (b), 157, 158, 165, 166 (t, b), 168 (b), 170 (t), 172 (r), 174, 174–75, 177 (l), 178 (b), 181, 182, 185 (b), 187 (t), 191 (t), 194 (bl, br), 201 (l). **Getty Images:** Richard E. Aaron/Redferns: 90–91, 92; Jorgen Angel/Redferns: 66 (t), 71; Juan Barreto/AFP: 172 (l); BBC Photo Library/Redferns: 48, 119; Dave Benett: 177 (r); Garry Brandon/Redferns: 145; Richard A. Brooks/AFP: 190; David Corio/Redferns: 110 (t); Fin Costello/Redferns: 150; Phil Dent/Redferns: 120–21, 126–27, 138; Ian Dickson/Redferns: 100, 102–03; David Warner Ellis/Redferns: 80, 81; EMI Archives/Redferns: 46–47; Evening Standard: 111; Matthew Fearn/AFP: 178 (t); Fotex Agentur GMBH/Redferns: 132, 146; Jon Furniss/WireImage: 198–99; GAB Archives/Redferns: 27, 28, 32, 38 (l), 58 (t), 104, 113 (r), 122 (l); GEMS/Redferns: 68 (l), 74 (t); Mick Gold/Redferns: 43, 86–87, 88; Jo Hale: 179; Nick Hale/Hulton Archive: 26–27; Tim Hall/Redferns: 147 (t), 152 (l); Patrick Hertzog/AFP: 142–43; Dave Hogan: 185 (t); Mick Hutson/Redferns: 154, 158–59, 160, 182–83; Wojtek Jakubowski/AFP: 200; JM International/Redferns: 173; K&K Ulf Kruger OHG/Redferns: 64–65; Keystone Pictures: 28–29; John Lynn Kirk/Redferns: 78; Neil Libbert/Redferns: 72–73; Jeffrey Mayer/WireImage: 79 (b), 89 (t); Tim Mosenfelder: 186; Stuart Mostyn/Redferns: 201 (r); Ilpo Musto/Redferns: 155 (t); Paul Natkin/WireImage: 115, 123; Michael Ochs Archives: 36–37, 42, 54, 82–83; Adam Osterman/WireImage: 196–97; Jan Persson/Redferns: 84–85; RB/Redferns: 77 (b); David Redfern/Redferns: 99 (t); Adam Ritchie/Redferns: 18, 20–21; Janek Skarzynski/AFP: 184; Jim Steinfeldt/Michael Ochs Archives: 141; Peter Still/Redferns: 105, 108, 109 (t), 112, 171; Tom Stoddart/Hulton Archive: 136–37; Jon Super/Redferns: 188–89; Mat Szwajkos: 192–93; Tracks Limited/Redferns: 62; Rob Verhorst/Redferns: 98, 117, 124–25, 129 (r), 140 (t), 144 (t), 164, 169; Chris Walter/WireImage: 30; Andrew Whittuck/Redferns: 22, 24, 25 (t), 44–45. **The Kobal Collection:** 40–41; Films Du Losange: 75; Jet Films: 56 (l). **London Features International:** 15, 16, 32, 34, 39, 55 (b), 60, 69, 70, 96, 101, 133, 167, 170 (b), 180–81, 187 (b), 195. **TopFoto:** 61, 76 (t); Marilyn Kingwall/ArenaPAL: 191 (b); PA: 149 (b), 151.

Fall River Press
122 Fifth Avenue
New York, NY 10011

ISBN: 978-1-4351-1772-3

Printed and bound in China

1 3 5 7 9 10 8 6 4 2

PINK FLOYD REVEALED

BY IAN SHIRLEY
FOREWORD BY JERRY EWING

FALL RIVER PRESS

CONTENTS

FOREWORD

'Our music is like an abstract painting. It should suggest something to each person,' Syd Barrett once told a reporter. The late, one-time frontman of Pink Floyd was spot-on. Pink Floyd's long and illustrious career has mapped out new and ever further-reaching soundscapes as their career has progressed. From the abstract, psychedelic quirkiness of their 1967 debut album *The Piper At The Gates Of Dawn* all the way through to the analytical overview of the channels of communication that coursed its way through 1994's *The Division Bell*, the band have challenged, questioned and ultimately thrilled listeners for 40 years.

The near hysterical fervour that greeted the decision of David Gilmour, Richard Wright and Nick Mason, who since 1985 had been Pink Floyd, to accede to the demands of Bob Geldof to reunite with their erstwhile colleague Roger Waters for 2005's Live 8 performance, over a decade after the band's name was attached to any recorded output, speaks volumes for Pink Floyd's legacy, a sumptuous tapestry draped over rock's effervescent body.

And yet it is somehow equally fitting that this unique and final overture was itself drawn to a perpetual close in an appropriately

English and subdued manner with the sad passing of, first, Syd Barrett, in July 2006, who had long retreated from the acid-fuelled Sixties limelight to Cambridge, from whence the band originally came, followed in September 2008 by Rick Wright's sudden and unexpected passing. As much as the final coming together by the perceived 'classic' Floyd line-up took place with little fanfare from the band themselves, so the passing of old colleagues was greeted with quietly dignified tributes.

Having interviewed Messrs Waters, Gilmour, Wright and Mason for *Classic Rock* and *Classic Rock Presents Prog* magazines over the years, none of this comes as much of a surprise. The band's disinterest in fame and all that follows it has been well documented in the music they have made. It is a suitably English approach from these progenitors of that quintessentially English of music genres, progressive rock.

And yet it is this reticence to make overtures to the media that has gone a long way in shrouding the story of Pink Floyd with the cloak of mythology. There have been books written about the Pink Floyd story but, here, *Record Collector*'s Ian Shirley has set about mapping the journey of this most prodigious of bands, from their early days as architecture students to the arena-packing colossus that was Pink Floyd for the last 20 years of an outstanding career.

And much like the music that the band has made, despite what you think you know, there's always something else to be discovered. Syd Barrett was right, you know.

Jerry Ewing

INTRODUCTION

Back in June 2003 I had the rare pleasure of interviewing Nick Mason face-to-face for what proved to be an abortive feature for the *Financial Times*. The interview was conducted at his Ten Tenths offices in Kings Cross, London, and as I waited to be ushered into his presence, I took time to admire one of his original double bass-drum kits – with 'Pink' on one and 'Floyd' on the other – that stood proudly in reception.

Ironically, rather than Floyd, the interview concerned his love affair with high-octane performance cars and he talked with passion and enthusiasm about the thrill of motor racing. When all was spoken and done he took me on a guided tour through his personal forecourt of around 40 rare and beautiful machines that included a Trabant! 'Do you know anyone who might want to buy it?' he asked. As a Pink Floyd fan I thought of stumping up the cash myself. To own a car that was once owned by Nick Mason was tempting, although in the back of my mind I knew that my wife would kill me. A Trabant might be suitable for a U2 photo opportunity but there was not enough room in the back for the kids….

The maddening thing about interviewing Mason about cars and motor racing was that I was desperate to ask him about Pink Floyd. I was a rabid fan of their early music and despite the fact that *The Dark Side Of The Moon* has sold over 30 million copies, the album represented to me breathtaking risk as well as musical purity. Sadly, the closest we got to the flame was a story of David Gilmour and he buying Ferraris in Italy and racing them back to England. It was ironic that in the flesh although Mason looked like a man more suited to making calculated decisions in a multinational boardroom (is anything *less* multinational than Pink Floyd?) he adored flying around corners at punishing speeds and taking instinctive risks in cars worth hundred of thousands of pounds. Of course, his career had also been conducted at high speed, where instinctive risks had started in 1966 with a bare chassis called Pink Floyd that ended up making him millions of pounds, enabling him to indulge his passion for speed.

That, in essence, is the appeal of Pink Floyd. Despite the millions of records, CDs, DVDs and concert tickets sold, they were always true to their music: from their early days under

Syd Barrett to the Waters'-dominated multimedia rainfall of *The Wall*. Of all of the psychedelic bands of the Sixties, Pink Floyd were simply the best. There is no point in splitting hairs and making comparisons as, despite Barrett writing two astounding pop hits in 'Arnold Layne' and 'See Emily Play', this was just a tip of a musical iceberg that extended below the waterline where the band would delight a hip crowd through extended improvisation. What other major artists of the Sixties and Seventies came from such a base? The Beatles, The Rolling Stones, The Kinks, The Beach Boys, Bob Dylan and The Who, to name a few, worked mainly within the parameters of short songs both live and in the studio; Led Zeppelin and Jimi Hendrix did stretch things out, but this was usually to accommodate extended guitar solos from genies of the plectrum. Pink Floyd had more in common with The Doors who balanced pop songs against extended suites where the guitar and organ were the principal instrumental tools. True, in Germany Can also favoured extended grooves with an experimental edge. But no progressive band, not even King Crimson, played with structure and the possibilities of sound as much as Pink Floyd. On 'Interstellar Overdrive' Barrett was moving away from Clapton, Hendrix and

Jeff Beck to treating the guitar as a means of electronic texture as well as a melodic instrument. Much has been made of Barrett's descent into incoherence and mental numbness, but we should celebrate the fact that unlike Hendrix, Jim Morrison, Ian Curtis, Kurt Cobain and Marc Bolan, Barrett did not die young but lived until the aged of 60. He was not totally caged by his mental illness, but was able to live alone, go to art galleries, watch TV or just pop down the shops for a packet of biscuits. He also had the last laugh; despite the many sightings and occasional door-stepping photographer a multitude of bands from XTC to Blur could refer to a concise body of work and – lest we forget – classic photos and images of his Sixties' prime.

What is astounding is that without Barrett Floyd were so sure footed. Of course, there must have been some extremely sweaty palms at those early gigs with Gilmour on guitar where they might have looked out at a small audience and wondered if it was all going to end sooner rather than later. Two attempts at writing pop hits failed, and recording in the studio without Barrett to lead them meant that they had to re-engineer a new musical chemistry with David Gilmour. Yet they did.

A Saucerful Of Secrets (1968) remains one of my most favourite albums because 'Set The Controls For The Heart Of The Sun' not only showed the way forward but is a hypnotic song built on the secure foundations of early extended pieces. It must be remembered that the band grooved like no other. Richard Wright's inventive organ drones and melody runs, Gilmour's incisive phrasing and extended explorations, Roger Waters' melodic and pliant bass and Mason's almost symphonic approach to rhythm became a cornerstone of their live performances for the next 10 years before they became their own pit band playing with military precision to accompany the train timetable that staging *The Wall* live demanded.

At the core of Pink Floyd was a musical chemistry that connected them to their audience in a similar way to the more blues-based Grateful Dead. This was achieved through revolutionary quadraphonic sound (a precursor to modern-day surround sound). With this technique, Richard Wright (and later, sound engineers) was able to 'walk' anything from footsteps to vocals around the venue, augmented by increasingly sophisticated lighting, projection and cinematic effects. Floyd were the first band to put the mixing desk in the middle of the auditorium at live concerts. As much as they invested money in presenting their live shows they never 'performed' in the traditional sense, with the spectacle of a lead singer flanked by an incendiary guitarist to arrest an audience, as did the likes of Mick Jagger or Robert Plant. On and off stage, from obscurity to growing international success, Floyd did their best to remain anonymous.

Their early move into film soundtrack work like *More*, *La Vallee* and *Zabriskie Point* was a natural extension. Even with Barrett on board, Floyd's music was about spirit, mood and atmosphere; paid soundtrack work allowed the band to use ideas and fragments of songs to accompany images. It also served to keep the creative juices flowing through frequent composition. It was, of course, in the studio that Pink Floyd were masters. Despite later fractures and disputes, their collaborative endeavours between 1968 and 1975 produced not just their finest work but some of the greatest albums of all time. *Meddle*, *Atom Heart Mother*, *Dark Side Of The Moon* and *Wish You Were Here* remain as fresh on the ear today as when they were recorded. Songwriting and performance aside, it was an obsession with sound that made these albums perfect.

What other band prepared an entire breakfast for the microphone and released it as part of a track? Clocks were recorded and new studio toys from effects pedals to rudimentary and then expensive production model synthesizers were used with glee. It was during this period that many of the memorable songs that became *The Dark Side Of The Moon* were developed and road-tested for over a year before being recorded.

Success did not change the music. It would have been easy to flounder on the rock of the good life after *Dark Side Of The Moon* but *Wish You Were Here* was almost a twin brother in height, size and sales. Even when the band began to fracture under the weight of Roger Waters' dominance, Floyd continued to make challenging and compelling music on *Animals* and *The Wall*. That this intense concept piece yielded a *disco-sounding* hit single still amazes me. *The Final Cut* was the point at which Waters went solo and Gilmour, finding the bridge empty, put on the captain's hat and took the helm. Despite acrimony during the Nineties in the wake of Barrett and Wright's deaths, the legacy of the music is all that matters.

After Mason, I interviewed one of the people who ran Ten Tenths and on my way out saw Mason being photographed sitting in a high-performance sports car. He looked in his element. But, as this book will show, he was a much better drummer than he was a gentleman racing driver. And he was an excellent gentleman racing driver....

Ian Shirley

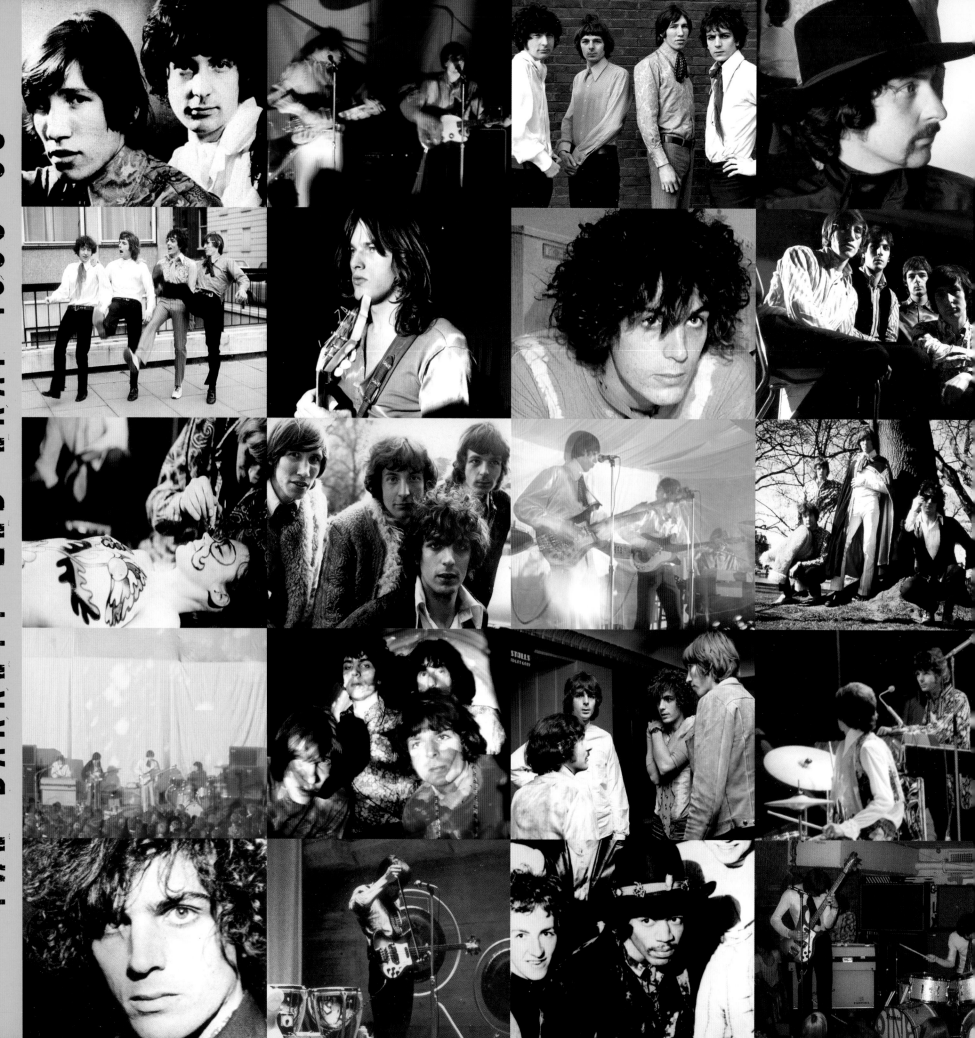

1965-68

Back in 1966, who would have thought that 43 years later Pink Floyd would be known around the world as one of the most musically, artistically and commercially successful bands in the world?

Roger 'Syd' Barrett (1946–2006), Roger Waters (b. 1943), Nick Mason (b. 1944) and Richard Wright (1943–2008) were an underground band whose experimental un-tethering of songs and passion for extended improvisation had more in common with jazz and experimental tangents than what was emerging in the wake of The Beatles and Bob Dylan as serious rock music. Even after signing to The Beatles label EMI in 1967, scoring two wildly successful psychedelic singles and recording an ambitious debut, their days seemed numbered despite groundbreaking ideas about quadraphonic sound and multimedia presentation.

Although Floyd had a healthy number of live bookings they were being pulled out of the pop cosmos into a dark black hole as girl-magnet, singer, songwriter and leader Syd Barrett began to unbuckle his senses and was no longer able to sing, write and lead. In early 1968 after a miserable American tour the previous autumn, Dave Gilmour (b. 1946) – who taught Barrett guitar chords as a teenager – was added, eventually replacing Barrett in the line-up on guitar and vocals. Despite failed singles Pink Floyd began to find their musical feet and, moving away from psychedelic pop songs, like the Grateful Dead in America, began the process of building a large devoted fan base, defining a style of music that would come to be known as 'space rock'.

1964-65
Origins Of The Band

Nick Mason first played drums in school band The Hotrods, 'retiring' when he went to study architecture in London at Regent Street Polytechnic. He was soon back in service with guitar-playing fellow student Roger Waters in Sigma 6 and a revolving line-up featuring a fellow former architecture-turned-music-student Richard Wright (if venues had a piano). By 1964/65, known as The Abdabs, The Screaming Abdabs and The Tea Set, they were playing pop, blues and R&B covers with Bob Klose (guitar), the strongest musician. Camberwell art student Roger 'Syd' Barrett joined and Klose left; when another band named Tea Set was discovered, Barrett came up with a name based on two blues players: Pink Anderson and Floyd Council.

1966
JANUARY: First Gig, London

The Pink Floyd Sound made their London debut at the Countdown Club in late 1965 and were paid £15 for their trouble. Their first London gig in 1966 took place at the Goings On Club on 9 January 1966. Like hundreds of other semi-professional bands around the country, Syd Barrett (guitar/vocals), Roger Waters (bass/vocals), Nick Mason (drums) and Richard Wright (organ) inflicted R&B covers like 'Louie Louie', 'Road Runner' and 'I'm A King Bee' upon a small audience. On jaunts around venues in Cambridge and London they occasionally shared bills with Joker's Wild featuring Barrett's friend Dave Gilmour (guitar).

MARCH - JUNE:
Spontaneous Underground

In February 1967, enthusiastic American organizer Steve Stollman began to promote a series of events at the Marquee Club in London, eventually under the banner of 'Spontaneous Underground'. Cream lyricist Pete Brown performed conjuring tricks as one of the attractions. In March Pink Floyd secured a residency and, legend has it, did not have enough material to play the contracted length and so began to extend songs by improvisation and musical experimentation. Interested fans included individuals like John 'Hoppy' Hopkins and Barry Miles (founder of Indica Gallery) who would shortly become instrumental in establishing the vibrant London Underground scene.

OCTOBER - NOVEMBER:
London Free School

During a series of fundraising dates at the London Free School's Sound and Light Workshop at All Saints Hall in Notting Hill Gate, Pink Floyd not only answered audience questions but were accompanied as they played by an American couple named Joel and Toni Brown who brought down a slide projector and put on a rudimentary light show. Already fascinated by the possibilities of combining visual arts with music, Pink Floyd began to add projectors and rudimentary lighting effects to their own concerts. Musically, the band had dropped covers in favour of self-penned songs and improvisations that were billed as 'space-age'.

OCTOBER:

All-Night Rave At The Roundhouse

John 'Hoppy' Hopkins and Barry Miles collaborated in establishing underground newspaper *International Times*. The launch party was held at The Roundhouse in Chalk Farm, London, on 15 October 1966. Two thousand guests, including Paul McCartney were entertained by music by The Soft Machine and Pink Floyd who had spotlights flashed on them in time to Nick Mason's drumbeats as they played extended tracks like 'Interstellar Overdrive' at such volume that the power failed. 'We find our audiences stop dancing now,' Roger Waters told a journalist from *The Sunday Times*, 'We tend to get them standing there, totally grooved with their mouths open.'

OCTOBER:

Sign With Jenner And King

Although gaining in sonic confidence the band's business arrangements for securing work were haphazard. This changed in the late summer of 1966 when the four members of Floyd formed a partnership called Blackhill Enterprises with lecturer Peter Jenner and his friend Andrew King. As managers, Jenner and King bought £1,000 worth of new equipment for the band, which was quickly stolen. Nick Mason's mother stepped in with £200 and the rest was bought on hire purchase. Blackhill also recruited 17-year-old Joe Gannon to improve and run live visual effects that now extended to slides, spotlights and coloured lights.

,DECEMBER: **UFO Club Debut**

Although the American psychedelic scene was already firmly rooted, London gained a focal point when 'Hoppy' and American producer Joe Boyd transformed an Irish dancehall in Tottenham Court Road every Friday night into the UFO Club. From the opening on 23 December 1966 Pink Floyd were the house band. Barrett had a growing armoury of curious yet lyrically pungent songs and open-ended jammed versions of 'Interstellar Overdrive' in which he would use echo effects or slide guitar. Rick Wright's pliant organ would mesmerize the audience, many of whom were discovering that LSD did not mean 'Lucy In The Sky With Diamonds'.

1967

JANUARY–FEBRUARY:
Early Recording Sessions

Working for the London arm of Elektra Records, Joe Boyd had already produced artists like The Incredible String Band. Peter Jenner and Andrew King had given him a rough Pink Floyd demo with a view to securing a deal. Although Elektra boss Jac Holzman did not go for the Floyd, Boyd, as musical director of the UFO, loved the band and arranged and produced their first recording session. Two Syd Barrett-penned tracks, 'Arnold Layne' and 'Let's Roll Another One' (later re-titled 'Candy And A Currant Bun'), were recorded over two nights in January 1967 at the four-track Sound Techniques studio.

MARCH:
Sign With EMI

The Boyd-produced sessions had been financed by the band's new booking agents who believed that 'Arnold Layne' (despite being about a man who stole ladies' knickers) was strong enough to secure a deal with a major label. There had been interest from Polydor, but EMI offered £5,000. This was accepted and Floyd – professional since February 1967 – invested in that most-important asset for the leading psychedelic band in England: a new Ford Transit van! Floyd still had to perform a 30-minute 'audition' for EMI, 'a futile exercise in our case,' wrote Nick Mason, 'since we had already signed'.

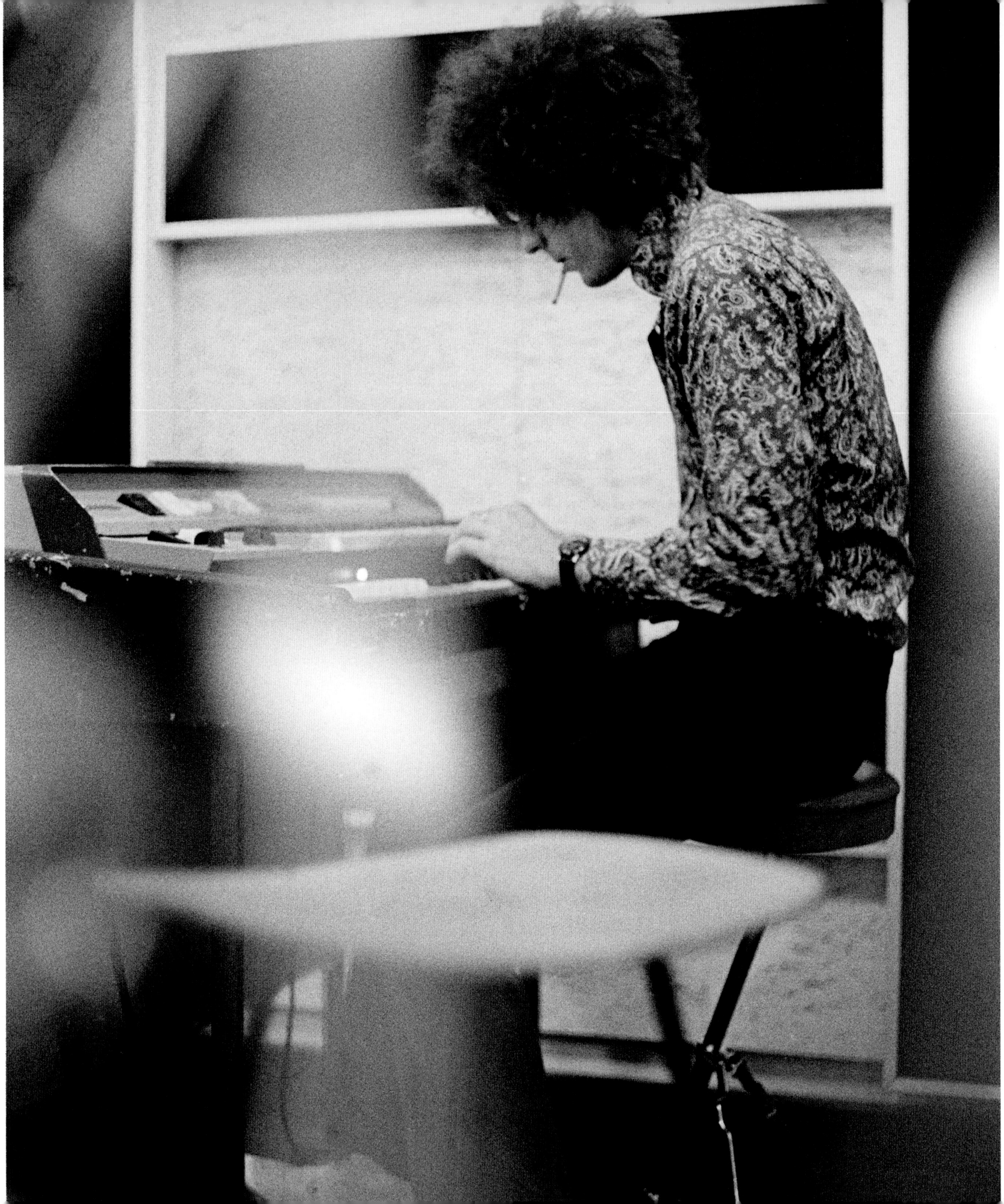

M A R CH: 'Arnold Layne'

The first Pink Floyd single 'Arnold Layne'/'Candy And A Currant Bun' was released to the world on 11 March 1967. Despite a partial radio ban due to lyrical content (it had a transvestism theme) 'Arnold Layne' reached the Top 20 in the UK charts. Concise, sharp and with delicious harmonies and a taut Richard Wright organ solo, 'Arnold Layne' rivalled The Kinks, The Who and The Beatles in turning pop singles into art-rock. There was later a promotional 'Arnold' film made of the band messing about on a Sussex beach with masks and a dummy.

APRIL: Technicolour Dream Concert

'Our music is like an abstract painting,' Syd Barrett told teen-mag *Trend*, 'it should suggest something to each person.' Combined with increasingly sophisticated lighting effects, Floyd were generating all manner of sonic ideas from the shadows with Barrett employing feedback, a Zippo lighter on his strings and a Bintone echo unit. Rick Wright's compelling organ drones and swells were underpinned by Waters' melodic bass and Mason's intuitive drumming often using softer tympani mallets instead of drumsticks. Their appearance at the end of the *International Times*' 14-hour long Technicolour Dream concert at Alexander Palace was their best gig – to date.

MAY: Games For May

Floyd's Games For May concert was held at the Queen Elizabeth Hall on 12 May 1967. Not only did they deploy slides and light, but projected film onto a white-screen backdrop. Even bubble machines were employed to make the event visually memorable. Tracks from their debut album were aired, including 'Bike', 'Pow R Toc H', 'Matilda Mother' and a new song, 'Games For May', which Barrett wrote specifically for the event; it would later be re-titled 'See Emily Play'. The band were then banned from the

venue after the bubbles and daffodils that were handed out to audience members soiled the upholstery.

JUNE: 'See Emily Play'

With their second single 'See Emily Play', Pink Floyd crossed the bridge from underground darlings to overground pop sensation. Floyd recorded the song at Abbey Road Studios but found that the finished result lacked the dynamism of the Joe Boyd-produced 'Arnold Layne'. They re-recorded 'Emily' at Sound Techniques, and it was this version that was released and went to No. 6 in June 1967. Syd Barrett even got to go on a 'blind date' to give his views on a number of new singles for *Melody Maker*; he found Jim Reeves' 'Trying To Forget' a 'very way out record'.

JULY:
Top Of The Pops

Floyd had been scheduled to appear on Top Of The Pops when 'Arnold Layne' first charted in March 1967 and the BBC had even filmed the band for broadcast. As the record dropped three places that week, the producer did not air the performance. With 'See Emily Play' eventually becoming a Top 10 hit in July 1967 the band appeared on this British pop institution three times with Barrett famously looking more dishevelled with each appearance. Sadly, the tapes of these appearances were accidentally wiped by the BBC in the early 1970s.

AUGUST:
The Piper At The Gates Of Dawn

Pink Floyd's debut album was recorded – aptly – at Abbey Road whilst The Beatles were still recording *Sgt. Pepper* (1967). Joe Boyd had wanted to produce but EMI insisted that their own engineer, Norman Smith, set the controls. Sessions went smoothly with Smith, a musician and former Beatles' engineer, helping to sharpen Floyd's unique sonar pencils. He also guided them towards the wealth of instruments and sound effects at their disposal in Abbey Road to add texture to their songs. *The Piper At the Gates of Dawn* was released on 5 August 1967. 'Astronomy Domine' and 'Interstellar Overdrive' gave a pungent flavour of their extended live explorations and Barrett's unique songwriting whimsy and angular vinegar on tracks 'Bike', 'Lucifer Sam' and 'Matilda Mother' were perfectly framed by the band's intuitive play.

AUGUST: Barrett's Mental State

The *News Of The World* had gleefully reported on the alleged excesses of the 'freakish' underground scene and a reference to Floyd being 'social deviants' had even delayed the signing of their EMI contract. Although the band experimented, it was Barrett who dived head-first into the acid pool. His reaction to the drugs he took led to erratic behaviour and began to impair his ability to perform, most notably at an Alexandra Palace gig where he stood motionless on stage, tripping. Gigs were cancelled in August 1967 with a press release giving Barrett's 'nervous exhaustion' as the cause.

OCTOBER – NOVEMBER:
First US Tour

Resuming live dates in September, Barrett's mental unravelling had a negative impact upon Floyd's first visit to America in October 1967. Showcase gigs on the West and East coasts ranged from good to near farce when Barrett might de-tune his guitar during a song or not sing. Flying in with only their guitars, the band had to borrow an organ and a set of drums for Rick Wright and Nick Mason to play. With Floyd billed as 'the light-kings of England', when manager Andrew King saw the high-powered displays used by some venues he diplomatically suggested they 'combine resources'.

NOVEMBER: US TV Appearances

Floyd made two TV appearances during their brief stay in the US. On *The Pat Boone Show*, when interviewed, Barrett's answers were confined to one or two words, although he did say 'America' when asked what he liked. On Dick Clark's *American Bandstand* the host showed the camera a copy of Floyd's debut album before introducing the band. Barrett either – consciously or unconsciously – didn't mime properly to their latest single, 'Apples And Oranges', although contrary to legend did answer two questions coherently in interview. Roger Waters answered the most important question as to what kind of American food they had enjoyed; 'two cheeseburgers'.

NOVEMBER - DECEMBER: Support The Jimi Hendrix Experience

Pink Floyd supported The Jimi Hendrix Experience on a package tour that took in venues as diverse as Chatham and Bristol over three weeks between 14 November and 5 December 1967. In reality, Floyd – a last-minute replacement for The Turtles – were limited to performing 17 minutes a night for two shows in order that headliner Hendrix and three other acts (The Move, The Amen Corner and The Nice) could strut their stuff. That Davy O'List from The Nice would have to deputize for Barrett, on one occasion (who could not even perform for 17 minutes) spoke volumes....

NOVEMBER: 'Apples And Oranges'

With Barrett's increasingly erratic ways, internal friction was inevitable. Outside London, audiences wanted to hear the two Pink Floyd hits and the more practical Waters and Mason wanted to oblige. Barrett wanted the music to roam freely at length but was mostly incapable of playing. To make matters worse, the third Pink Floyd single 'Apples And Oranges' was released on 18 November and flopped. Not that Barrett was bothered. 'Couldn't care less,' he told *Melody Maker*, 'All we can do is make records which we like.' Spookily he was predicting the future direction of Floyd – without him.

DECEMBER:
Christmas On Earth Continued Concert

Pink Floyd played around 200 shows during 1967 and wrapped up the year in the company of Hendrix, Eric Burdon and The Animals, The Soft Machine and others at the ambitious all-night Christmas On Earth Continued concert at Kensington Olympia on 22 December. The Who failed to turn up; Syd Barrett was on stage when Floyd appeared amongst large geometric shapes to reflect their lights, but neither his guitar nor he was plugged in. Furious, Waters, Mason and Wright soldiered gamely on with – allegedly – Davy O'List playing in the wings. This could not go on.

1968
JANUARY: David Gilmour Joins

With Barrett's unreliability profoundly affecting the band's ability to make money by fulfilling live obligations, his old friend Dave Gilmour was drafted in as a backup guitarist. His previous bands Joker's Wild, Flowers and Bullitt, had failed to make an impression and he was delighted, albeit with natural reservations over Barrett's feelings. In January 1968 Pink Floyd became a five-piece band – for a handful of gigs. As Barrett wrote and sang most of Floyd's material there was talk of him becoming a Brian Wilson figure; a non-performing creative studio force, but new Barrett material was fractured and disjointed.

LEWES F.C. PRESENTS NON-STOP
SWINGING '68 1000 WATT FREAK-OUT
LEWES TOWN HALL
THE FANTASTIC MIND BLOWING
LIGHT SHOW
★ OF THE
PINK FLOYD
PLUS
★ **GRANNYS INTENTIONS**
(DERAM RECORDS)
★ AND JOHNNY FINE AND THE RAMBLERS
FRIDAY 19ᵗʰ JANUARY
7.45 to 12.00 midnight   BAR EXTENSION TO 11.0   ADMISSION 12.6

JANUARY:
Tonite Let's All Make Love In London

Tonite Let's All Make Love In London was a semi-documentary film directed by Peter Whitehead, first shown in 1968, that served to analyze the social phenomenon that was 'swinging' London. For Floyd fans, images of John Lennon wandering around in a sheepskin coat are secondary to glimpses of Floyd performing. As Nick Mason uses mallets to circulate around his tom toms, sitting on a chair with his guitar on his lap Barrett is not playing the instrument but coaxing shards of rainbow-sounding texture to colour what many fans consider to be one of the greatest recordings of 'Interstellar Overdrive'.

JANUARY: Band Splits From Barrett

That Syd Barrett's last live appearance with Pink Floyd was at the end of Hastings Pier on 2 January is sadly fitting. Although his feet were physically on the ground, he was mentally all at sea. Famously, on the way to their next gig his fellow band-mates simply decided not to pick him up. His 'departure' from the band was officially announced on 6 April 1968, although by that time Pink Floyd were touring and recording without him. The Blackhill Partnership dissolved, with Jenner and King opting to continue working with the creative element of the band: Barrett.

Steve O'Rourke

Floyd sought out new management at the Bryan Morrison Agency where Steve O'Rourke (far right) had already been handling their affairs with regards to concert bookings. Indeed, he had provided Gilmour with a room and tape recorder to learn the Floyd songbook when the guitarist joined the band. O'Rourke was be Floyd's manager until his death in 2003, taking care of all their business matters from employing members of their road crew for their increasingly sophisticated lighting and visual presentations to negotiating concert bookings and Alan Parson's rates as an engineer! Like Nick Mason, O'Rourke had an absolute passion for motor sport.

MARCH – APRIL:

'It Would Be So Nice'

On 10 February 1968, *Record Mirror* reported that 'Corporal Clegg' was going to be Floyd's next single. Despite inspired wah-wah guitar from new boy Gilmour and a delicious kazoo break, Waters' Lennon-esque tale of a soldier losing a limb in the Second World War was rejected. Richard Wright sang on his own 'It Would Be So Nice' that failed to chart. The band were regrouping and remapping their future. 'Single releases have something to do with our scene,' Waters told *Melody Maker*, 'but they are not overwhelmingly essential. On LPs we can produce our best at any given time.'

ΜΑΥ: *The Committee* Soundtrack

With extended pieces that ranged from intense to hypnotic, Pink Floyd had been creating soundtrack music live that, when they had control over the venue, was best experienced in a multimedia, cinematic environment. Post-Barrett the band recorded segments of score music for the art film *The Committee* (1968). Written by Max Steuer, directed by Peter Sykes and featuring Paul Jones from

Manfred Mann in the main role, the film had a limited release and it was not until it was unearthed and released on DVD in 2005 that Floyd's movement to the light in this medium was generally heard.

⚡UₙE: **Hyde Park Free Festival**

Despite two failed singles, Barrett was still considered luminous by fans unaware of his condition, and there was speculation that Floyd would flounder without him. Instead, without a focal point they began slowly to turn lead into gold through live performance where the texture of the music became even more of a focal point. Headlining on the last day of the Hyde Park Free Festival on the 29 June 1968 was a critical and personal breakthrough, with soundscapes like 'A Saucerful Of Secrets' engaging the crowd. Even DJ John Peel (left) – mainly there to see his beloved duo Tyrannosaurus Rex – loved them.

⚡UₙE: *A Saucerful Of Secrets*

A Saucerful Of Secrets (1968) was in many respects Floyd's second debut album. The one song recorded with Barrett – 'Jugband Blues' – was pointedly placed at the end of the album, allowing the new songs, like Waters' gorgeous 'Let There Be More Light' and the cinematic musical textures of Richard Wright's 'Remember A Day', to emboss themselves into listeners' minds. Roger Waters was emerging as an unlikely source of powerful songwriting; his rolling mini-suite 'Set The Controls For The Heart Of The Sun' was swiftly to become a live Floyd anthem and saw their music labelled as 'space rock'. This despite the *New Musical Express* reviewer finding the track 'long and boring', with 'little to warrant its monotonous duration'. *Saucerful* was also notable for being only the second album where EMI allowed an artist to hire and pay outside designers. Floyd's friends Storm Thorgerson and Aubrey Powell as the Hipgnosis design team answered only to Floyd and at £105 were not paid as much as Peter Blake (£200) who conceived The Beatles' *Sgt. Pepper* album cover. Around this time Pink Floyd renegotiated their contract, agreeing to reduce their royalty rate from eight per cent to five per cent in return for unlimited studio time.

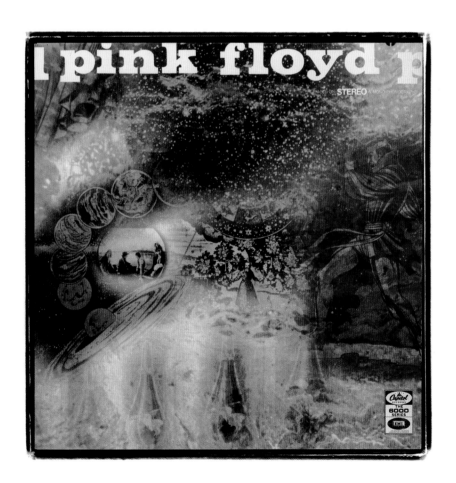

JULY – AUGUST:
A Saucerful Of Secrets Tour

Dave Gilmour later admitted that when he first came into the band he was trying to play 'like Syd'. As UK and European gigs piled up between May and June 1968 his creativity as a guitarist began to mesh into the musical forests of 'Astronomy Domine' and 'Interstellar Overdrive'. Floyd returned to America in July to cover ground missed previously due to visa issues and Barrett's obscure behavior. Once again, they arrived with hardly any equipment but Jimi Hendrix allowed them to take whatever they wanted from his newly constructed Electric Lady recording facility. Although the Floyd set list still rested heavily upon early material 'Set The Controls For The Heart Of The Sun' began to find its feet as a concert favourite. 'Arnold Layne' and 'See Emily Play' were noticeable by their absence.

DECEMBER: 'Point Me At The Sky'

At the time of its release on 17 December 1968 no one knew that 'Point Me At The Sky'/'Careful With That Axe, Eugene' would be the last Pink Floyd single to be released in the UK for 11 years. Musically pungent and an inventive blend of instrumental and vocals, no one but the likes of John Peel would give 'Point Me At The Sky' – penned and sung by Waters and Gilmour – radio needle-time. B side, 'Careful With That Axe, Eugene' was written and recorded in a three-hour session; an expanded version became a staple of the band's live set over the next few years.

THE COLLABORATIVE ERA: 1969-75

1969-75

If Pink Floyd had disbanded in the wake of Syd Barrett's mental unravelling, they would be remembered today alongside Tomorrow and July as cult bands thrown up by the psychedelic era, releasing one fantastic album and a clutch of singles before fading from the light. With Dave Gilmour on guitar, however, *A Saucerful Of Secrets* revealed a deep well of musical creativity, collaboration, determination and, as well as short songs, a thrilling future direction based upon extended pieces like 'Set The Controls For The Heart Of the Sun'.

As a live act between 1969 and 1975 Pink Floyd would pioneer revolutionary sounding, lighting, staging and cinematic ideas that are now the norm for all major bands, irrespective of genre. Despite growing success in the UK, Europe and America the band remained personally anonymous rarely speaking to the music press and, unlike their early Seventies peers The Rolling Stones, Led Zeppelin, The Who and David Bowie, spent more time shopping for T-shirts than courting publicity through exotic social lives, hard living or questions over their sexuality.

Typically, in 1970 a picture of a cow rather than the band was pasted on a 12-m (40-ft) billboard in America to promote the album *Atom Heart Mother*. In the studio, now producing themselves, through albums and soundtrack work, Floyd would reach a creative peak with the ambitious elements of *Atom Heart Mother* (1970), *Meddle* (1971), *Obscured By Clouds* (1972), the seminal *The Dark Side Of The Moon* (1973) and stellar *Wish You Were Here* (1975).

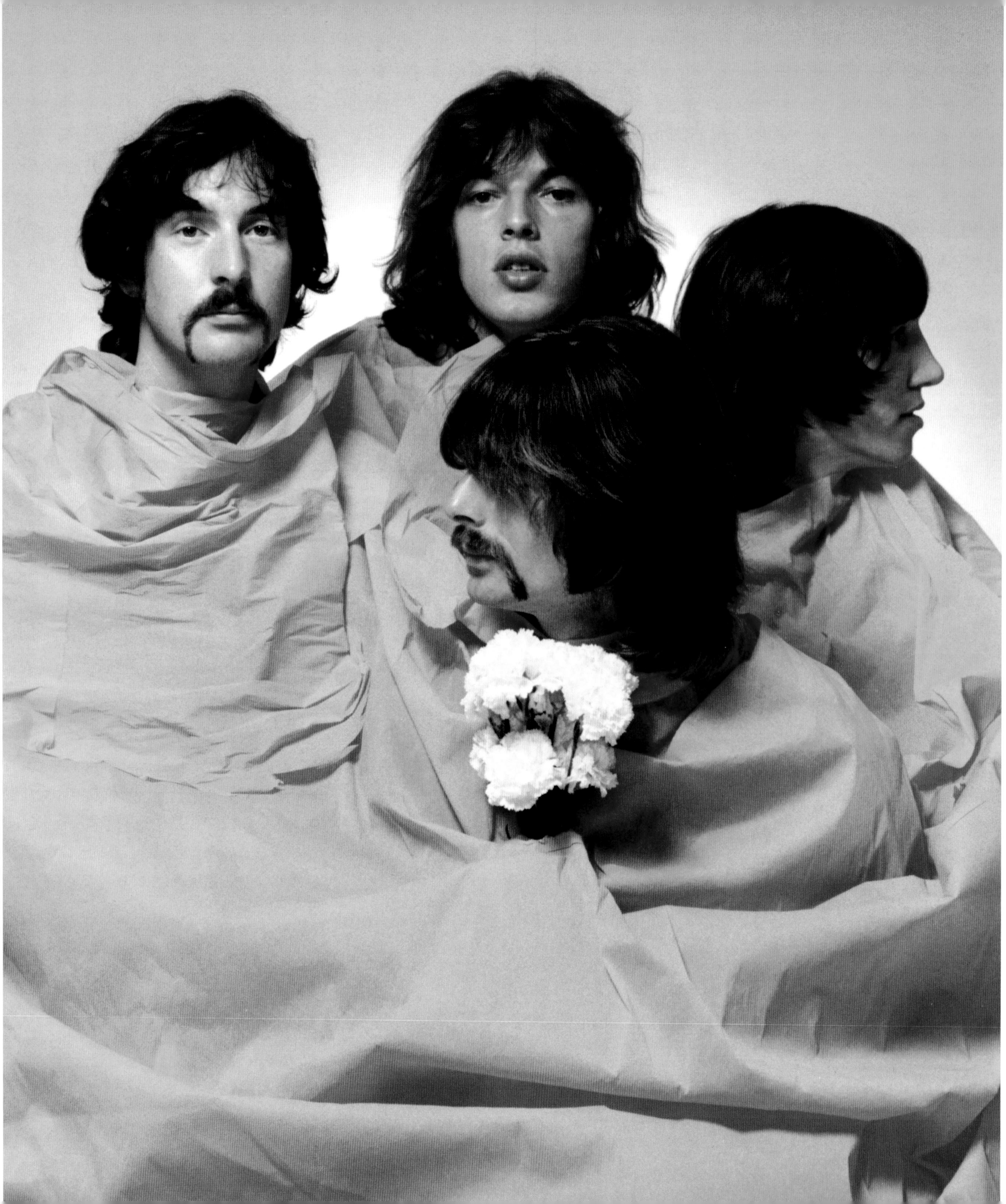

1969

APRIL:

The Massed Gadgets Of Auximenes Concert

Floyd's fascination with the quality of sound reproduction saw them invest money in equipment. At the Games For May concert in 1966 they pioneered a rudimentary quadraphonic sound with speakers placed at the *back* of the concert hall. By early 1969 they had a system constructed called 'The Azimuth co-ordinator', which received its own billing at performances and allowed sound generated by the band in performance as well as tapes to be moved around the auditorium by Richard Wright. At the Royal Festival Hall on 14 April Pink Floyd were no longer playing music but applying *aural wallpaper* to the environment.

MAY-JULY:

The Man/The Journey Tour

Floyd's 12-date UK tour between 16 May and 26 June was billed as 'concerts in 360 degree stereo', culminating in a performance at the Royal Albert Hall. This was attended by fans drawn to the compelling cinematic music flowing out of the band, who were delivering an ambitious extended 'concept' piece entitled 'The Man/The Journey'. Along with the band taking afternoon tea on stage, new material was performed – of which the compelling Waters-penned 'Nightmare' ('Cymberline') was a highlight – as well as old material dressed up in different titles. 'Beset By Creatures Of The Deep' was, in fact, 'Careful With That Axe, Eugene'.

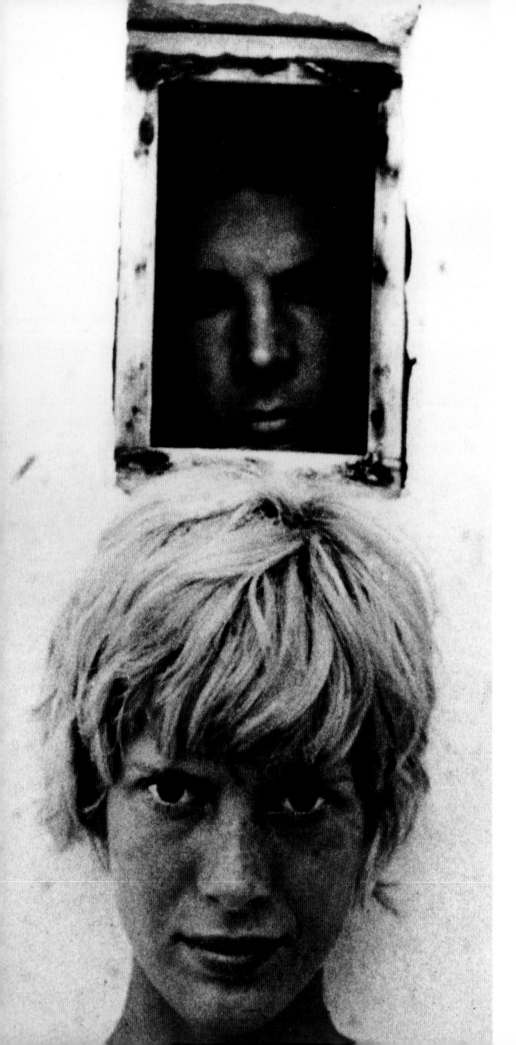

JUNE:
Soundtrack From The Film More

Whereas the music for *The Committee* was only heard by the small numbers who could find a cinema that showed the film, Floyd's soundtrack music for *More* was given an official release by EMI. Floyd's contribution was recorded over a week – five sessions – in February 1969 and ranged from the proto-punk of 'The Nile Song' to the dreamy, drifting birdsong of 'Cirrus Minor'. 'Doing the music for films is a very challenging thing,' Rick Wright told *Top Pops And Music Now* magazine, 'We have to express facts and scenes in music.' The album went Top 10 in July.

OCTOBER: *Ummagumma*

Floyd's soundtrack work broke the traditional wheel of consecutive album releases. Their official third outing *Ummagumma* was a double and released on 25 October 1969. The first disc presented extended live airings of tracks like 'Astronomy Domine', 'Careful With That Axe, Eugene', 'Set The Controls For The Heart Of The Sun' and 'A Saucerful Of Secrets'. Waters told a *Melody Maker* journalist that 'Interstellar Overdrive' was not on the album as the band 'didn't dig' the recorded version, although the plan to press and distribute 2,000 acetates for fans who wanted to hear it never materialized. The second LP explored a new frontier of experimentalism with each band member presenting solo pieces. Waters presented two, the reflective 'Grantchester Meadow' previously aired live as part of the 'The Man/The Journey' concerts. Wright's four-part keyboard opus and Mason's treated drum tattoo showed how confident the band had grown with the possibilities of the recording studio. On 'The Narrow Way' Dave Gilmour played everything from guitar to drums well although sung like a man who hoped no one was listening.

PINK
FLOYD

1970

JANUARY:

The Madcap Laughs

Syd Barrett's debut solo album *The Madcap Laughs* was released on 3 January 1970. Assisted, in part by Dave Gilmour, Roger Waters, bass player Jerry Shirley from Humble Pie, Willie Nelson from Quiver and even members of The Soft Machine it had been recorded at considerable expense over numerous sessions mainly due to Barratt's inability to focus. Some tracks were constructed on the loose rope bridges of Barrett's un-metric acoustic guitar parts and singing. Like Captain Beefheart's equally idiosyncratic *Trout Mask Replica* (1969) gold was struck on compelling tracks like 'Terrapin' and 'Dark Globe'. The goodwill that Barrett retained meant reviews were positive and strong for this collection of off-centre but appealing songs. 'I like to have really exciting, colourful songs,' he told a journalist from *Melody Maker* and when he spoke to *Record Mirror* was drawn to comment on *Ummagumma*, 'The singing's very good and the drumming is good as well.'

JANUARY:

Zabriskie Point Soundtrack

Pink Floyd's third soundtrack project was recording some tracks for Italian director Michelangelo Antonioni's film on American counterculture *Zabriskie Point*. In the studio for two weeks the band were confronted with a perfectionist. 'We had each piece of music and we did about six takes of each, and he'd choose the best,' Rick Wright told *Beat Instrumental* magazine. Many thought that Pink Floyd's music would have suited Stanley Kubrick's *2001* (1968) especially the psychedelic death/ rebirth at the end of the film. When Kubrick wanted to cut and use a segment from 'Atom Heart Mother' for *A Clockwork Orange* (1972) Waters refused.

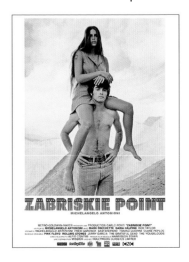

APRIL–MAY: US Tour

Ummagumma began to provide Floyd with an audience in America, and in April 1970 the band returned to undertake the first of two tours that year. In San Francisco, manager Steve O'Rourke hired Bill Graham's Fillimore West to ensure the set-up of lights and sound by Floyd's growing road crew was perfect. Floyd dispensed with support acts whose equipment got in the way of Mason's impressive barrage of tympani, percussion instruments and gong which Waters would theatrically attack during performance. Shows were played in Los Angeles and Atlanta before their equipment – valued at £15,000 – was stolen in New Orleans. Luckily the boyfriend of a girl in the hotel Floyd were staying worked for the FBI and quickly located the equipment, allowing the tour to continue.

JUNE:

Extravaganza '70 – Music And Fashion Festival

Although Syd Barrett's record label gently coaxed him into a couple of interviews to promote *The Madcap Laughs* and the single 'Octopus', anything else was an uphill task. A live tour was out of the question, although Barrett did perform in the studio for John Peel's *Top Gear* accompanied by Dave Gilmour on bass and Jerry Shirley on drums. He also made a fleeting appearance with the pair at the London Extravaganza '70 – Music And Fashion Festival playing 'Terrapin', 'Gigolo Aunt', 'Effervescing Elephant' and 'Octopus' before deciding to put down his guitar and walk off the stage into the wings.

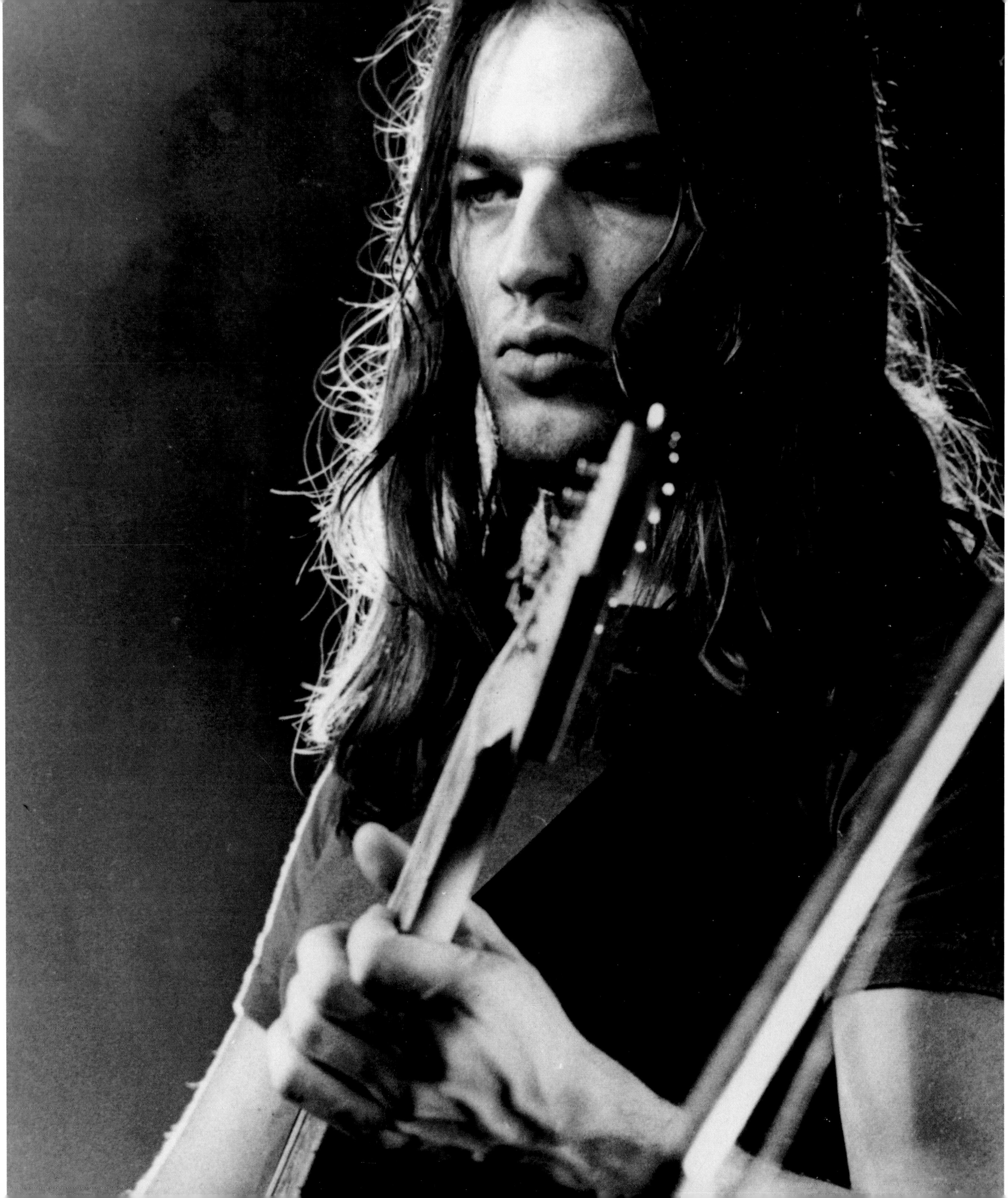

JUNE: Bath Festival

Led Zeppelin were the headline act for the Bath Festival of Blues & Progressive Music held at Shepton Mallet, Somerset, on the weekend of 27–28 June 1970. Floyd stole the show, coming onstage at 3 a.m. on the 27th due to festival organizational delays. After playing stage favourites like 'A Saucerful Of Secrets' and 'Set The Controls For The Heart Of The Sun', Floyd were augmented by a brass band and choir to reward the audience with a 'special pudding'. This 'Epic' new piece would later be titled 'Atom Heart Mother'. A firework display set the seal on a perfect performance.

JUNE: Rotterdam Pop Festival

As bootlegs and YouTube footage confirm, a day after playing at the Bath Festival, Floyd delivered a fantastic hour-and-a-half set at the Kralingen Pop Festival in Holland. A 20-minute version of 'A Saucerful Of Secrets' which Rick Wright knew so well by then he could drink from a bottle of beer as he played his Hammond M102 organ, captivated an audience, some of whom danced around a bonfire as the music washed over them. 'Atom Heart Mother' received its second official public performance.

JULY:
Second Free Hyde Park Concert

Although Syd Barrett had not delivered the golden egg they expected, Blackhill Enterprises had expanded into promotion, and staged the second free Hyde Park Concert under the banner of Blackhill's Garden Party on 18 July 1970. In front of over 50,000 people Floyd topped the bill over Kevin Ayers, Lol Coxhill, The Edgar Broughton Band and Roy Harper. Musically, the band captivated the late-afternoon crowd with staples like 'Set The Controls For The Heart Of The Sun' and 'Careful With That Axe, Eugene'. Somehow the 'Atom Heart Mother' choir and brass band managed to cram onto the small festival stage.

SEPTEMBER:

Atom Heart Mother World Tour Begins

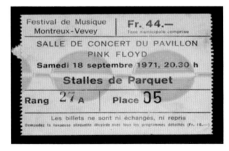

The title of the 'Atom Heart Mother' suite was inspired by a newspaper article about the potential of a woman receiving a nuclear-powered pacemaker. Floyd gave themselves a financial heart attack by hiring a choir and brass players in order to recreate faithfully the suite live. This was in addition to their quadraphonic sound, which allowed footsteps and other musical effects to be walked around auditoriums by Richard Wright. It was estimated that Floyd lost £2,000 per performance on the *Atom Heart Mother* tour, although American audiences were swelled by increasing numbers of fans discovering this ultimate 'space rock' band.

OCTOBER: *Atom Heart Mother*

In later years Waters, Mason, Gilmour and Wright commented that the suite on one side of the *Atom Heart Mother* LP was a failed experiment. In fact, this collaboration with composer Ron Geesin who had previously worked with Roger Waters on *The Body* soundtrack (1970), is a fine piece of work and was re-aired in live performance by Geesin and Gilmour at the Chelsea Festival on 14 and 15 June 2008. Its original studio genesis had been tortuous, with Floyd laying down the basic track and Geesin adding arrangements over the top while they were on tour. Geesin – and later John Aldiss – added textures, brass and a full choir to complete one of the era's best examples of symphonic rock. The acoustic waft of Waters' 'If', Dave Gilmour's 'Fat Old Sun' and Richard Wright's Beach Boy Floyd of 'Summer '68' confirmed the strength of songwriting in the band and the effects-laden 'Alan's Psychedelic Breakfast' was Floyd at their most playful. The album cover designed by Hipgnosis of a cow in a field with no band credit was design genius, helping *Atom Heart Mother* become Floyd's best-selling yet.

NOVEMBER:

Barrett's *Barrett*

Whilst Pink Floyd were winning a worldwide audience Syd Barrett was gently slipping into oblivion. Released in November 1970 *Barrett* was his second album in a year. Although tracks like 'Gigolo Aunt' and 'Baby Lemonade' sparkled, many others were cobbled together from whatever was left over from *The Madcap Laughs* sessions and what his record label and assorted Floyd helpers could get out of him to construct musical frames around. Barrett was now living in Cambridge and although he did some coherent press interviews was now having more mentally cloudy than clear days.

1971

MAY: *Relics*

1971 opened with the release of the *Relics* compilation, which was a pert summary of Floyd's progress to date with the stellar Barrett singles 'Arnold Layne' and 'See Emily Play' sitting comfortably alongside later work like Waters' 'Cirrus Minor' and 'The Nile Song' from the *More* soundtrack. The sleeve for *Relics* was drawn by Nick Mason, revealing that his architectural training had not gone to waste. In fact, as they could not write music Mason and Waters would plan the cartography of extended Floyd performances by drawing maps and diagrams, planning peaks, troughs and quiet passages of play.

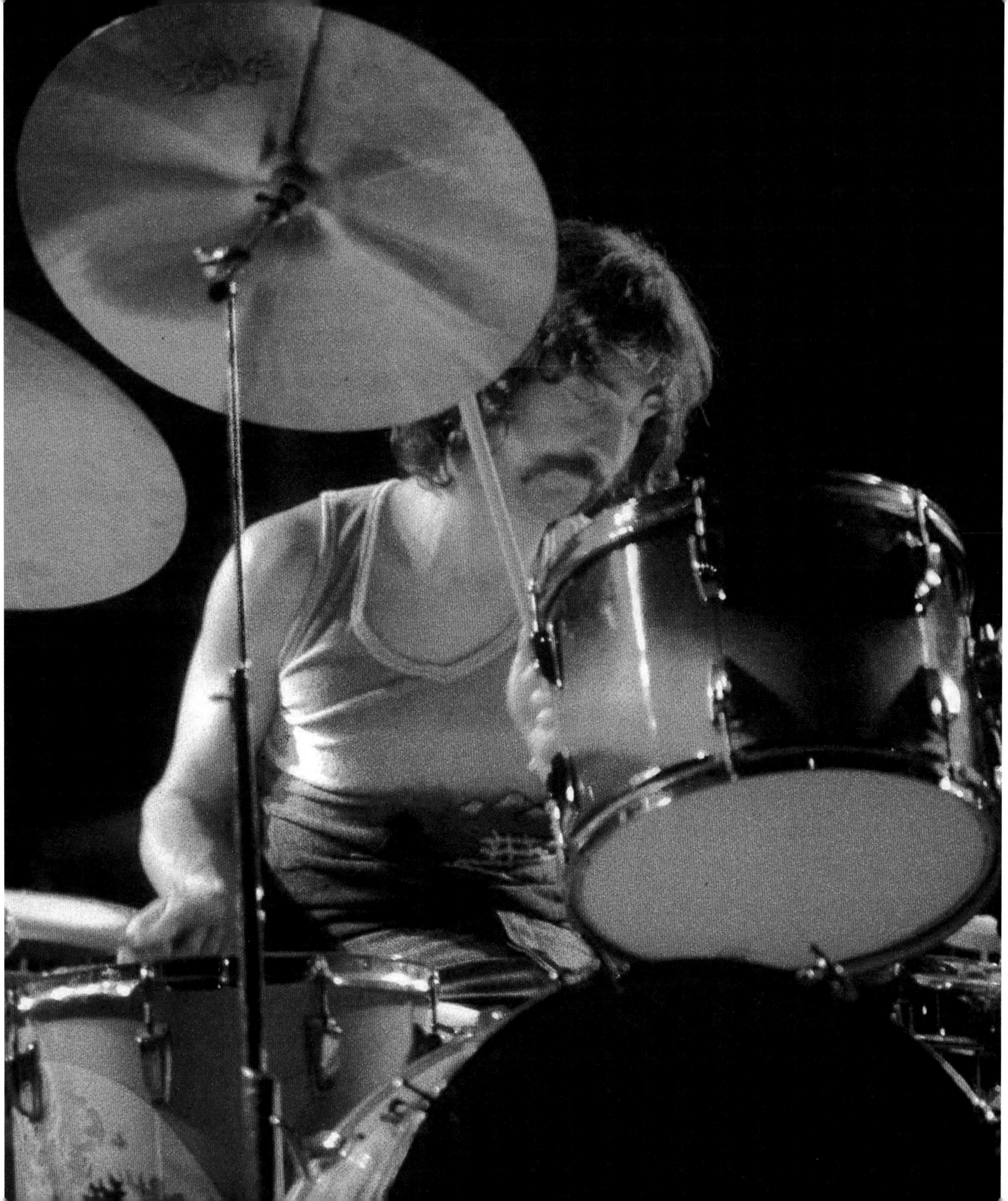

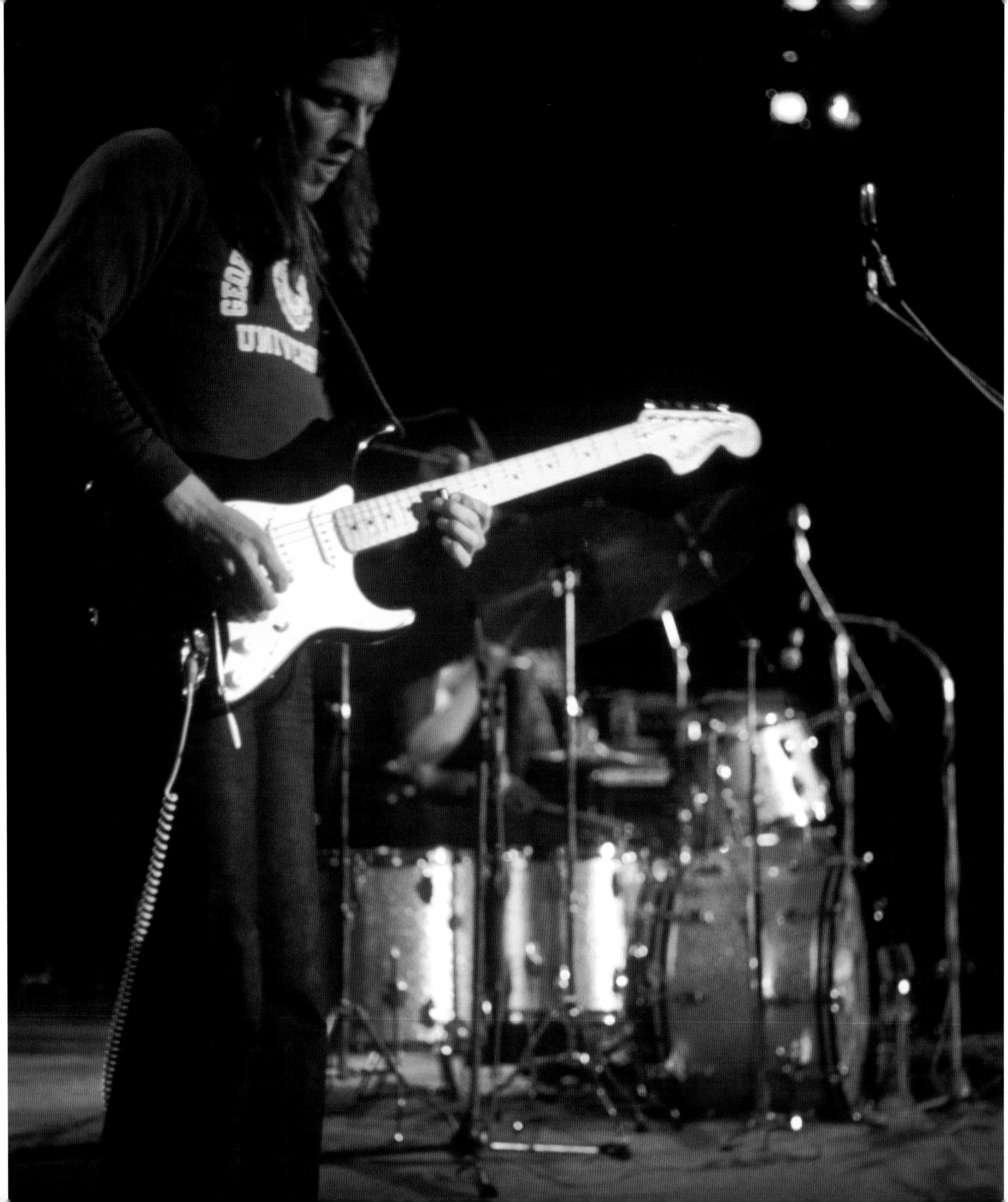

AUGUST: Far East Tour

Unlike their contemporaries Led Zeppelin, The Who and The Rolling Stones, Floyd were not prone to on-the-road excess. Lists of instruments, equipment and just how they got their live quadraphonic sound were more likely to appear in the press than tales of red snapper redeployment or hotel room reconstruction. They were hardly recognized on the street; the main personality of Pink Floyd was the music, as demonstrated between 6–15 August 1971 where they embarked upon their first Far East tour consisting of three dates in Japan and two in Australia where, at one venue, only 500 people turned up.

OCTOBER: *Meddle* Tour Begins

In a revealing interview with *Melody Maker* published on 9 October 1971, Roger Waters confessed to a journalist that the band had actually begun to rehearse again, 'I can't remember the last time we had a rehearsal. I think that often the cause of groups splitting up is when people freak and can't come up with new stuff, which has happened to us.' On the *Meddle* tours (Europe: 18 September–11 October and America: 15 October–20 November) the extended track 'Echoes', originally titled 'The Return Of The Son Of Nothing', was first performed live.

OCTOBER: *Meddle*

Sessions for *Meddle* (1971) commenced in Abbey Road Studios in January 1971 and continued, where time permitted, during their hectic 1971 tour schedule. During that first session Rick Wright was playing around on a piano amplified through a Leslie speaker. When Wright hit a single note on his keyboard that sounded like a sonar ping, the ears of the rest of the band pricked up. Repeated, this note formed the introduction to one of the most famous Pink Floyd pieces of all time – 'Echoes' which took up the entire second side of this Top 3 album. 'One Of These Days' is one of the greatest-ever opening tracks on any album. Throbbing bass ostinato, howling winds, pulsating rhythm, an early proto-techno interlude, Wright's keyboard splashes, Gilmour's guitar howling like a high-performance car before taking off into a stratospheric solo and even a *Doctor Who* reference condensed into under six minutes! The wistful acoustic prowl of 'A Pillow Of Winds' and 'Fearless', featuring an extended 'sample' of the Anfield Kop football crowd are also memorable. The price for such consistent innovation was paid on the howling-dog blues of 'Seamus'.

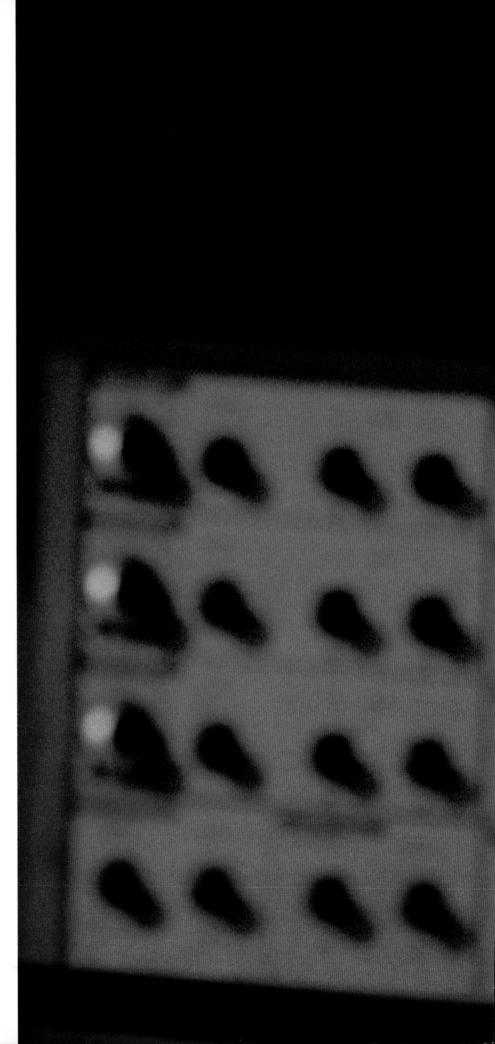

1972

FEBRUARY:

Barrett Resurfaces With Stars

Like the banquet ghost at Shakespeare's *Macbeth*, Syd Barrett continued to manifest himself at unlikely times, even appearing one day at Abbey Road Studios in 1971 when Ron Geesin was working on sections of 'Atom Heart Mother'. In 1972, he was encouraged by former Tomorrow drummer 'Twink' (above, far right) to form a three-piece band including bass player Jack Monck under the banner of Stars. Two support slots at the Cambridge Corn Exchange on 24 and 26 February 1972 baffled the crowd as Barrett stumbled through the set with one apparent lyric: 'Hay, hay, Saturdays in the hay.'

JUNE:

Obscured By Clouds

The recording of the soundtrack to Barbet Schroeder's *La Vallee* (1972) where a young French couple embrace native life of New Guinea took place in late February/early March 1972 in the Strawberry Studios at Chateau D'Herouville, France. Instrumental pieces were taut and the uncomplicated beauty of vocal tracks

like 'Burning Bridges' and the almost Rex-tacy of 'Free Four' revealed a Floyd delighting in the simple pleasures of short rock songs. When released in June, the album was titled *Obscured By Clouds* due to the strength of the opening track which began to be incorporated into the band's live set.

mike kaplan presents
Bulle Ogier
in
Barbet Schroeder's
The Valley
obscured by clouds
X
Music
Pink Floyd
Michael Gothard
Jean-Pierre Kalfon
Valerie Lagrange
and The Mapuga Tribe and its Chiefs
Photography: Nestor Almendros Sound: Jean-Pierre Ruh Filmed in Techniscope in Papua-New Guinea
Written & Directed by: Barbet Schroeder

SEPTEMBER:

Pink Floyd: Live At Pompeii

Floyd's dream of appearing in a feature film was realized in September 1972 when *Pink Floyd: Live At Pompeii* was premiered at the Edinburgh Festival. The band had been filmed performing tracks like 'A Saucerful Of Secrets', 'Echoes' and 'Careful With

That Axe, Eugene' in the old Roman amphitheatre over four days between 4–7 October 1971. There was no audience to allow the camera crew's full unfettered licence and with the breathtaking backdrop, results were stunning. Other segments and tracks like 'On The Run' and *Dark Side* taster 'Brain Damage' were filmed in a Paris recording studio in 1972.

1973

J A N U A R Y:

Le Pink Floyd Ballet

Pink Floyd's collaboration with ballet producer Roland Petit was first mooted in 1970, and Dave Gilmour and even Floyd's manager Steve O'Rourke had talked enthusiastically about working with a 106 piece orchestra and the world-famous dancer Rudolf Nureyev. When performed for French TV on 14 January 1971 the dancers moved to 'Set The Controls For The Heart Of The Sun' and 'Careful With That Axe, Eugene'. Petit re-staged the ballet in 1973 and this music was used again as was 'Echoes' and 'Obscured By Clouds'. Part of the first performance was broadcast on French TV on 14 January 1973.

MARCH:

The Dark Side Of The Moon Tour Begins

Pink Floyd embarked on two extensive US tours in 1973. The first opened at the Dane County Memorial Coliseum in Wisconsin on 4 March and these 16 dates ended on 24 March 1973 in Atlanta, Georgia, the day their new album *The Dark Side Of The Moon* was released Stateside. The band were augmented by three backing singers and Gilmour's former Joker's Wild band-mate Dick Parry whose saxophone was a vital part of the track 'Money'. After three UK performances Floyd returned to the States for a further 13 stadium dates. As well as quadraphonic sound, the visual spectacle that included dry ice, flares, rising platforms, mobile spotlights, strobes and lasers was equal to old favourites like 'Obscured By Clouds' and the breathtaking music from their latest album.

MARCH:

The Dark Side Of The Moon

Fittingly, the world premiere of *The Dark Side Of The Moon* was held at the Planetarium in Baker Street, London, a location the Floyd had always wanted to use as a venue. Sadly, Floyd only appeared as four cardboard cutouts in reception, although Rick Wright was in attendance. The album was played to journalists in the Planetarium itself, although their positive reviews meant little as *Dark Side* took on a life of its own as fans and even those who had not previously been into the band were eager to hear this seminal album. Musically, this reflection on the pressures of life was a *tour de force*. From the stately 'Breathe' and 'The Great Gig In The Sky' to the sprightly torque of 'Time'

every track was – and remains – a classic. Hipgnosis's cover art – the famed rainbow prism – matched the sheer genius inside. One (rejected) cover idea was to feature Marvel Comics' Silver Surfer riding a wave, to emulate the *Crystal Voyager* film shown during live Floyd performances, Storm Thorgerson said in 2003.

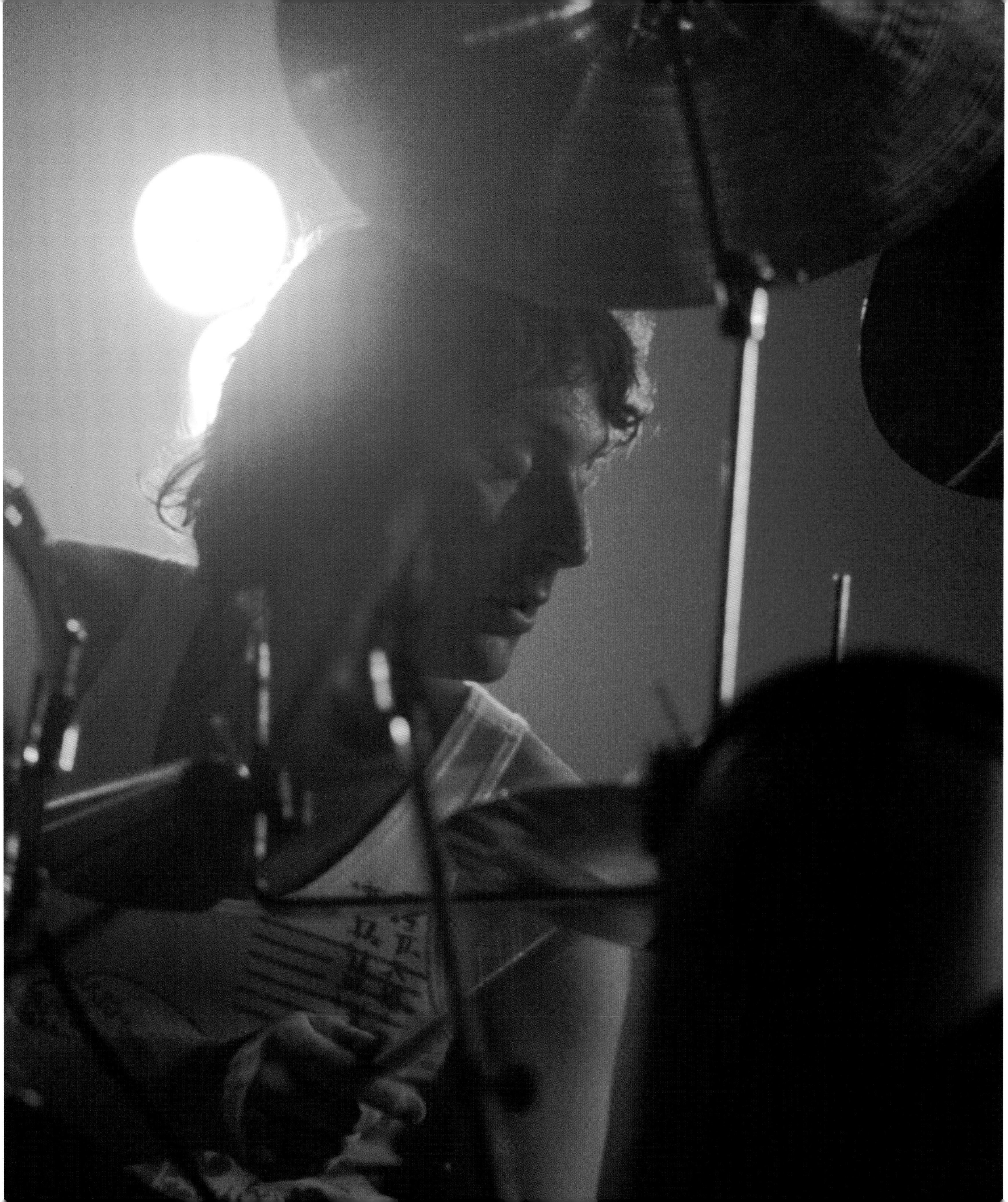

☧ A ☧: 'Money'

Although *Dark Side* shot to the top of the American album charts, Capitol wanted Floyd to break the AM Top 40 radio market and this meant releasing a single. As Floyd considered themselves an albums' band and had not released a 7-inch since 1968, they had to be persuaded by the label and manager Steve O'Rourke. The band relented and 'Money'/'Any Colour You Like' reached the US Top 20 in June. Floyd experienced a sense of 'See Emily Play' *déjà vu* when, during the second leg of their US tour, new fans would scream out 'Money!' demanding to hear the hit as soon as possible.

☧ A ☧: Spectacular Effects

Pink Floyd were originally scheduled for one performance at London's Earl's Court arena on 20 October, but the 20,000 seats sold out so fast that a second date was added on the 19th. With typical thoroughness the sound team attended a David Bowie concert the week prior to Floyd's appearance just to get a feel for the acoustics. On Floyd's two nights a huge balloon was inflated to resemble the moon and special effects extended to a flaming gong and an aeroplane crash landing on the stage during the second half of the show.

OCTOBER:
Household Objects Sessions

One of the most endearing stories in Pink Floyd history is their post-*Dark Side* experiments aimed at writing songs based on sounds created by common household objects. One imagines Roger Waters twanging elastic bands or Nick Mason attacking his drum kit with two toilet brushes in the pursuit of inspiration. Experiments were abandoned three (partial) songs in, although Nick Mason did tell a journalist from *Sounds* in 1974 that post-*Dark Side*, 'the *Household Objects* album would have been the wittiest thing to do next, and it would have been if we could have knocked it out'.

NOVEMBER:

Robert Wyatt Benefit Concerts

At the *International Times*' launch Floyd had shared the bill with The Soft Machine whose own art-rock explorations had won a smaller audience. After three albums drummer and singer Robert Wyatt (left) departed to lead his own band Matching Mole. On 1 June 1973 he fell from a third-floor window in Maida Vale and was paralyzed from the waist down. Floyd agreed to perform at a benefit concert at the Rainbow Theatre on 4 November. Floyd delivered two half-hour shows of *The Dark Side Of The Moon* at 5 p.m. and 9 p.m. DJ John Peel, who compered the show, estimated that £10,000 was raised.

DECEMBER: *A Nice Pair*

In the wake of *Dark Side* EMI were quick to grab the Floyd 'cow'
by the udders, and re-issued the first two albums as *A Nice Pair*.
American label Capitol were more than happy: *Dark Side* had
been their last contracted album before Pink Floyd moved to CBS
Records, despite all manner of entreaties to stay. Hipgnosis were
also delighted with the commission as they gleefully adorned the
artwork with all manner of visual puns and a selection of possible
covers. The release again raised interest in Syd Barrett, who

 now had his own fan club, prompting
a lengthy article in the *New Musical
Express* penned by Nick Kent.

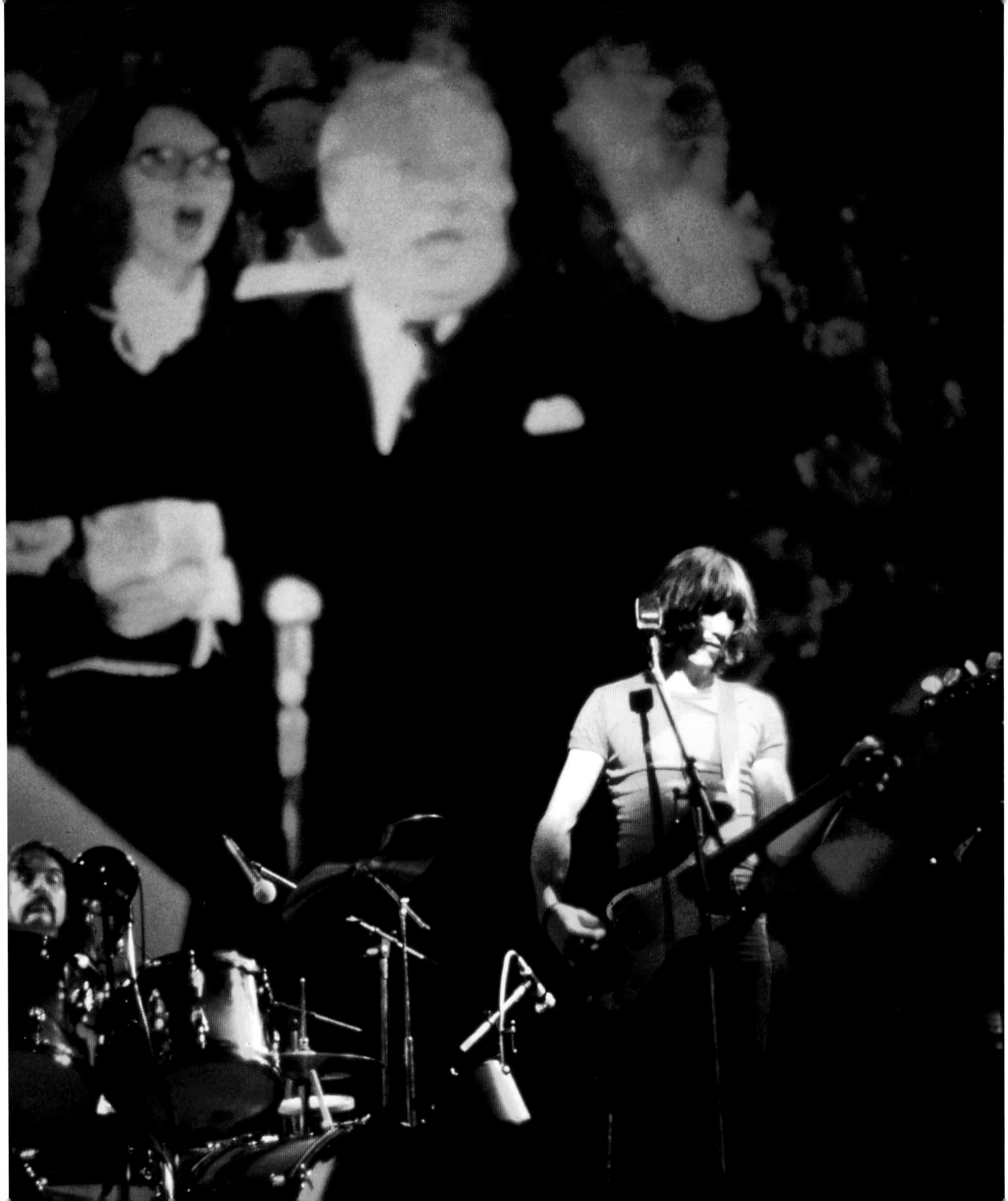

FRIDAY JUNE 20 8:30 PM
THREE RIVERS STADIUM

**PINK
FLOYD**
1975

No Bottles, Cans,
or Alcoholic
Beverages
Permitted in the Facility

ADVANCE TICKETS
Available at all
NATIONAL *Record Marts*

1974

NOVEMBER–DECEMBER:

British Winter Tour

Despite their success and heavy touring schedule, the individual
members of Pink Floyd kept amazingly low profiles. The only
member who went anywhere near excess was Nick Mason, who
had inherited a passion for performance cars from his father and
began to build up his own collection. Any wild sexual activities
were conducted behind closed doors by Waters, Mason and
Wright – with their first wives! When they did give press interviews
there was usually serious discussion about music, instruments
and the equipment employed to stage Floyd's increasingly
elaborate live shows. In 1974 the band only ventured out of
the recording studio for some summer European dates and
a short UK tour that ran from 4 November to 14 December.

1975

APRIL:

Wish You Were Here Tour Begins

Pink Floyd's 1975 tour was confined to North America, with
an additional date headlining the Knebworth Festival in England.
As well as debuting 'Shine On You Crazy Diamond' and 'Have
A Cigar' from their upcoming album, *Wish You Were Here*, they
also deployed a new Roger-Waters designed, pyramid-based
stage which had a revolutionary inflating *Dark Side* top that was
intended to rise into the air during performance. Sadly, wind was
a problem and on 20 June in Pittsburgh the band were, in Nick
Mason's words, 'like Captain Hornblower faced with an out-of-
control mainsail'. The floating pyramid was cut free and landing
in a car park was ripped up by souvenir hunters.

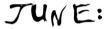

JUNE:

Barrett Arrives At Abbey Road Studios

With 'random precision' during the final mixing session for *Wish You Were Here* at Abbey Road Studios on 5 June 1975 the band received an unlikely visitor: Syd Barrett. Waters, Mason, Gilmour and Wright failed to recognize him at first as their former leader had put on so much weight and shaved both his head and eyebrows. Barratt probably killed conversation stone dead when he announced that he was ready to contribute to the band again. Ironically, Barrett's replacement Dave Gilmour had got married that morning and after attending the wedding reception in the Abbey Road canteen Barrett did not return.

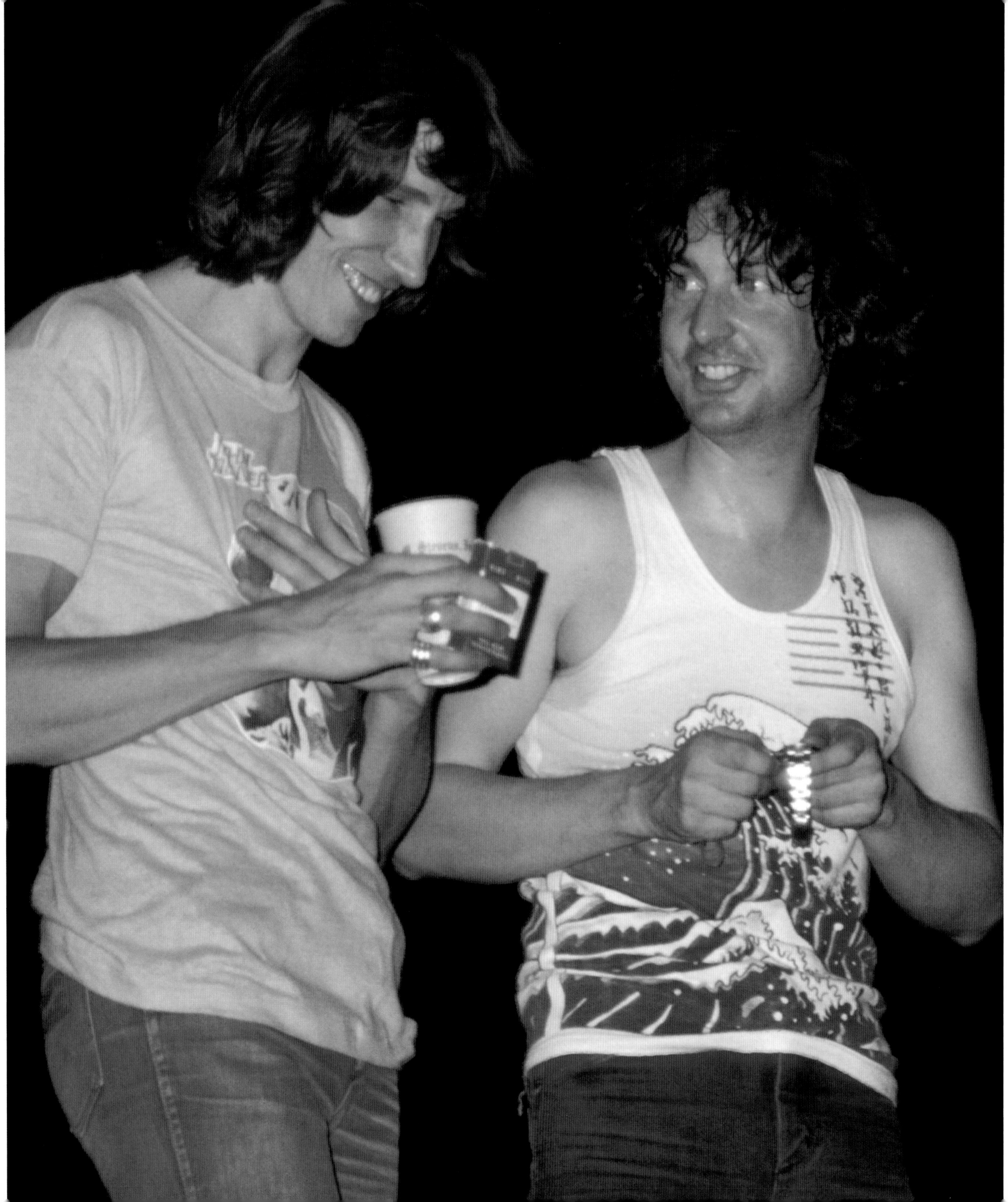

JULY:

Knebworth Festival

Pink Floyd's headline appearance at the Knebworth Festival on 5 July 1975 took place in good weather in front of an estimated 100,000 people. The live premiere of the *Wish You Were Here* material was marred by the sound balance having to be rushed in order that two Spitfires could fly over the crowd as a sound

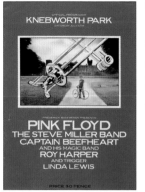

effect at the opening of the track 'Breathe'. The band (not the Spitfires) were late for their cue and the first part of the set was below par. The ship was back on course for the second half, during which the band simply nailed *The Dark Side Of The Moon*.

SEPTEMBER:

Wish You Were Here

If the ghost of Syd Barrett haunted Pink Floyd, it also served as inspiration when the band finally got down to work on the follow-up to *Dark Side*. *Wish You Were Here* was dominated by the sonic suite of 'Shine On You Crazy Diamond', a fitting tribute to their former leader. Arranged in two parts, it was musically astounding with Gilmour's famed opening guitar solo leading into a four-note guitar hook serving as one of many compelling strokes on this bold musical canvas. Lyrically, in 'Part One' Waters managed to define everything that represented the Syd Barrett legend now and then in 17 lines.

THE WATERS-LED ERA: 1976-85

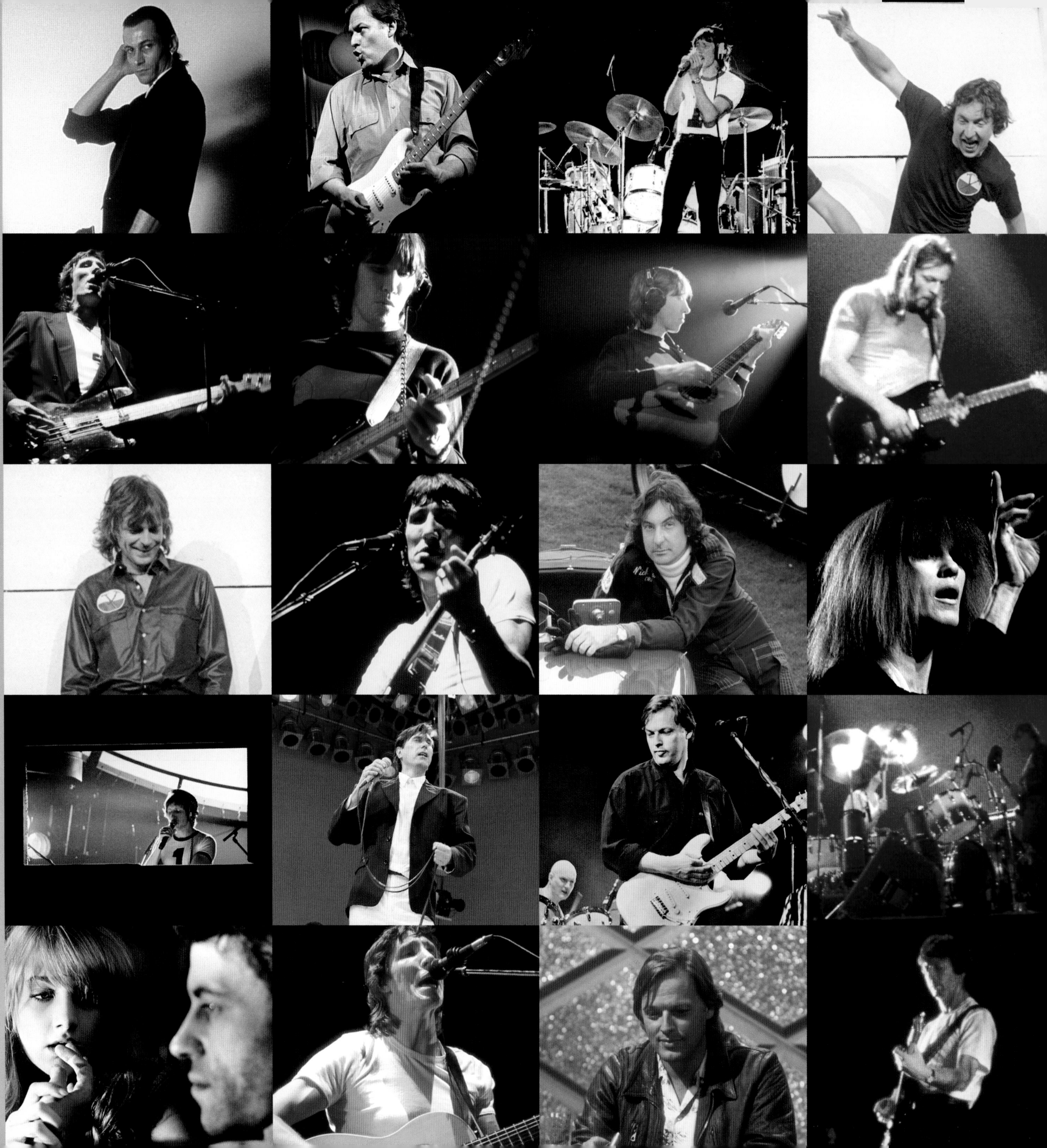

1976-85

The period 1969–76 was highly collaborative, with all four members of Floyd making a contribution to the process of writing musical material or coaxing ideas to fruition in extended studio sessions or during live performances. Roger Waters had, though, emerged as the prime lyricist in the band and his passionate nature and strongly held convictions guided both his musical and thematic ideas.

Despite *The Dark Side Of The Moon* spending years in the UK and US album charts bringing Floyd huge financial rewards and packed stadia, Waters was not creatively becalmed. From *Animals* (1977) onwards he dominated proceedings to the extent of taking control not only of overall production duties on *The Wall* (1979) and *The Final Cut* (1983) but also using outside co-producers like Bob Ezrin as musical sounding boards instead of fellow band members. By *The Final Cut* a number of session musicians were being deployed to provide the instrumental textures or arrangements that his vision required.

Waters' lyrical barbs against society, war, politics, morality and hypocrisy were countered by emotional sensitivity unlocked by the early loss of his father. *The Wall*, as an album, tour and film, was one of the greatest and most complete multimedia events pulled off by Floyd, even if Waters had forced Rick Wright out of the band during its long studio gestation. Ironically, when he officially decided to go solo he was confronted by Dave Gilmour and Nick Mason, steely-eyed and prepared to sail onwards as Pink Floyd – without him.

1976

DECEMBER: Battersea Photoshoot

Roger Waters' idea for the cover of the new Pink Floyd album was of a pig hovering over the four chimneys of the Battersea Power station. He tasked Hipgnosis to photograph this concept. A 12-m (40-ft) inflatable pig was duly made and inflated, and three days were set aside in December – even with the album scheduled for release in January – to allow the photograph to be taken. The pig was filmed on the first day and became untethered on the second, allowing Roger Waters, air-traffic controllers over Heathrow Airport and police helicopters to confirm that pigs really could fly.

1977

JANUARY: *Animals*

Like the flying inflatable pig Floyd, too, had become untethered from their usual working practices. In 1976 they had upgraded their rehearsal space in Britannia Row, Islington, into a 24-track studio and between April and November laid down and mixed *Animals*. Two tracks that had previously been aired live as far back as 1974 ('Gotta Be Crazy' and 'Raving And Drooling') formed the basis for 'Dogs' and 'Sheep'. As sessions dragged on, Waters' lyrical themes, combining allusions to George Orwell's *Animal Farm* (1945) and his own cynicism with the failings of capitalism, and political and moral authority, came to dominate proceedings. Musically, the album was as barbed and direct as *Meddle* had been dreamy and allusive. The sonic torpedoes were book-ended by two short Waters haiku entitled 'Pigs On The Wing Parts 1 and 2', which may have seemed out of place but formed his best love song since 'Stay' on *Obscured By Clouds*.

JANUARY – JULY:

In The Flesh Tour

Although the Pink-Floyd touring beast was well-oiled to the extent of travelling with their own generators, a 10-m (32-ft) back projection screen, a 5-m (17-ft) tower to show Ralph Steadman cartoons commissioned specifically for the tour, a giant glass flower and huge human inflatables they fell foul of the Greater London Council (GLC) when preparing the *In The Flesh* concert at Wembley Empire Pool in London. Their fears that the inflatable pig may become untethered (again) annoyed Roger Waters who now took the lead role in choreographing performances. Sound engineer Brian Humphries told *Melody Maker* that he preferred the floating porker to the aeroplane crashing into the stage, 'Funnily, the GLC gave us fewer problems over that than this pig.'

JULY:

Spitting Incident

When the punk-rock movement emerged in London in the summer of 1976 some audience members showed appreciation by spitting at bands. Roger Waters turned this on its head on the final gig of Floyd's 1977 American tour in Montreal by spitting in the face of a member of the audience. That Waters now actually felt personal animosity towards his mass audience after a decade of touring was the germ of the entire *The Wall* concept. Saying that, when discussing the event with radio DJ Tommy Vance in 1979, Waters – perhaps unwittingly – mixed up the role of the protagonists: 'What he wanted was a good riot', he said, 'And what I wanted to do was a good rock and roll show.'

1978

Tax Exile

Album sales and tour receipts made Pink Floyd one of the most financially, as well as commercially, successful bands in the world. Due to pungent UK tax laws that would take up to 83 per cent of all income – leaving them with 17 pence from every pound earned – they were eventually advised to seek shelter by living overseas. Rick Wright was the first to go into financial exile, moving to the Greek island of Rhodes and Roger Waters later moved to Los Angeles. The band could spend a proportion of time in the UK but would, in future, have to plan recording sessions around their accountant's tax-planning strategies.

MAY: *David Gilmour*

In June and July 1978 Dave Gilmour gave a series of rare interviews to promote his debut eponymous solo album (which had been released in May of that year). Although questions probed the guitarist about Floyd's working practices and future plans, Gilmour was more comfortable discussing the musical reunion with two former Joker's Wild members – Rick Willis (bass) and Willie Wilson (drums) who appeared on this warm album with him. The album sold well in America and the UK and Gilmour told one journalist why there was something missing in each sleeve: 'I've never been keen on my lyric sheets because I'm not sure that my lyrics stand up.' Which is nonsense, as 'Fat Old Sun' and 'Mudmen' show.

$\mathcal{J}\mathcal{U}\mathcal{L}\mathcal{Y}$: **New Material**

In September 1977 Roger Waters had begun to write a batch
of new songs that were set down as rough demos at his home
studio from January 1978. When he presented them to the rest
of the band in the summer he had songs for two concept pieces:
'The Wall' and 'The Pros And Cons Of Hitch Hiking'. After much
discussion the band opted for 'The Wall' concept. 'The basic
structure was there,' Nick Mason was to recall in later years,
'like a skeleton with lots of bones missing.' Preliminary work
in adding flesh started at Britannia Road Studios in
November 1978.

Richard Wright

Wet Dream

1979

SEPTEMBER: Wright's *Wet Dream*

Although Dave Gilmour's solo album sold well on the back of his promotional interviews, Richard Wright's *Wet Dream* failed to dent even the lower reaches of the chart when released in September 1978. Not that Wright, the most laid-back and reclusive member of Floyd was bothered. The title had less to do with sexual matters than Wright's enjoyment of sailing his new yacht in Greece. The light cocktail jazz feel of tracks like 'Mediterranean C', 'Cat Cruise', 'Waves' and 'Mad Yannis Dance' were a million miles away from the strident sound of *Animals* and the growing Waters-led claustrophobia surrounding Pink Floyd.

OCTOBER: Wright Resigns

With Waters and co-producer Bob Ezrin driving *The Wall* sessions in Los Angeles, New York and France Floyd were no longer operating as a unit. Waters later stated that only Gilmour was of any musical use with Wright and, to an extent, Mason missing in action. Whether Wright was emotionally burned out after marital problems or simply non creative became moot points when Waters engineered his removal from the Pink Floyd partnership. That this could come to pass – and that Mason and Gilmour would agree – revealed how dysfunctional Floyd had become. Amazingly, Wright became a salaried musician for *The Wall* performances.

NOVEMBER:

'Another Brick In The Wall (Part 2)'

The last Pink Floyd single released in the UK had been 'Point Me At The Sky' in 1968 which had sunk without trace. The track 'Another Brick In The Wall (Part 2)', with its sub-disco beat, guitar, funky feel, an impromptu choir of school children whose classroom was just down the road from Brittania Row, was seen as a perfect way to raise the curtain on *The Wall* album. Despite Waters' caustic lyrics questioning the benefits of education, it rocketed to the top of the charts when released on 16 November. The feat was repeated in America in January 1980.

NOVEMBER:
The Wall

The Wall was the concept album to end all concept albums. This song-story was hatched by Roger Waters and based around the character Pink partially to reflect extremes of his own life and experiences with a sprinkling of Syd Barrett thrown in for good measure. Themes of loss, megalomania, delusion, oppression, war, paranoia and – at heart – an artist's relationship with his audience made for a cracking four sides of vinyl. Passion, intent and fine music literally bled from the speakers with tracks like 'Comfortably Numb', 'Hey, You' and 'Is There Anybody Out There' becoming some of the most memorable of all Floyd's sub-five-minute songs. Like Beethoven's Ninth Symphony, *The Wall* is the monumental brick in Waters' own artistic wall.

1980

FEBRUARY: *The Wall* Tour Begins

The Wall in concert remains one of the most visually spectacular shows staged by any rock band. The concept of a 340-white-brick wall 49 m (160 ft) wide and 10.5 m (35 ft) high being erected as the band performed to collapse at the finale was a stroke of theatrical genius. With staggering effects, including giant inflatable puppets and the obligatory crashing aeroplane as well as film, lights and Gerald Scarfe going hammer and tongs at the animations *The Wall* could not be toured in the traditional sense and was performed only 29 times at indoor venues in Los Angeles, New York, London and Dortmund. Extensive band rehearsals were required – and additional players were brought in – for performances where lights, effects, images and music were synchronized to military perfection.

1981

MAY: *Nick Mason's Fictitious Sports*

In May 1981 Nick Mason became the third Floyd member to release a solo album when *Nick Mason's Fictitious Sports* was released. 'Fictitious' was something of a pun as the main writer of the jazzy tracks was pianist and composer Carla Bley (above). 'I wanted to make a record of stuff that I like, by musicians that I like, in which I played a hand in putting together,' Mason told *International Musician* in July 1981, although he was peeved that there had been a delay of 18 months from the album being finished until it was released. Musically, a garden fence rather than a wall...

JUNE: Final Performance With Waters

Although Roger Waters would later tour *The Wall* as a solo artist its last performance by Pink Floyd took place at Earl's Court in June 1981. These five shows were staged specifically for the proposed *The Wall* movie which, at that moment, proposed to have footage of the band playing as narration. Amazingly, all the footage, including material shot by a crane that rose over the wall every night to show the audience, was deemed unsatisfactory. Although no one knew it at the time, this was Waters' last performance with Gilmour, Wright and Mason until the Live 8 concert in 2005.

NOVEMBER:

A Collection Of Great Dance Songs

To cash in on the success of *The Wall* EMI released *A Collection Of Great Dance Songs*. This strangely named compilation contained a version of 'Money' which, the lack of, was much in the thoughts of Floyd and manager Steve O'Rourke. Between 1972 and 1979, Floyd had invested a large proportion of their earnings with investment firm Norton Warburg who had speculated in a number of ventures and allegedly mismanaged their finances. Floyd were reported to have lost over £1 million and this financial can of worms also interfered with future tax planning. *The Wall* tour also lost money....

1982

The Wall Movie

Gerald Scarfe's unique form of art provided animations for segments of the *In The Flesh* tour as well as knocking the Hipgnosis design team off the front cover of *The Wall* album. With Roger Waters intent on taking the adventures of Pink to the screen he and the artist put together a 40-page illustrated storyboard – some of which were signed – to attract potential financial backers. After a false start, Alan Parker took up the reins of director and swiftly weaned Waters away from playing Pink himself, in favour of charismatic Boomtown Rats' lead singer Bob Geldof. Pointedly, Parker insisted Waters take a six-week 'holiday' during filming so that the director would not have to contend with artistic interference. Waters was present during the editing process where the live action, Scarfe's arresting animation and music were blended together – when they were not arguing – into a stunning realization of Waters' original idea.

JULY:

Pink Floyd The Wall Premiere

Pink Floyd The Wall had its world premiere at the prestigious Empire Theatre in London's Leicester Square on 14 July 1982. The three main creative sparks behind it, Waters, Parker and Scarfe, were all in attendance as were Nick Mason and Dave Gilmour. Bob Geldof (below, right) was also there to witness his wholehearted performance, as was actor Bob Hoskins who played the juicy role of his manager. Reviews were favourable and retrospect reveals *The Wall* as the first feature-length MTV video.

1983

MARCH:

Waters Wins BAFTA

Outside of music polls and top figures for touring box-office grosses, the members of Pink Floyd were not well-versed in winning prestigious awards. This changed in March 1983 when 'Another Brick in The Wall (Part 2)' won Roger Waters a BAFTA for Best Original Song, pipping 'The Eye Of The Tiger' from *Rocky III* to the post. *The Wall* also won a BAFTA for Best Sound, beating *Blade Runner* and *E.T.*

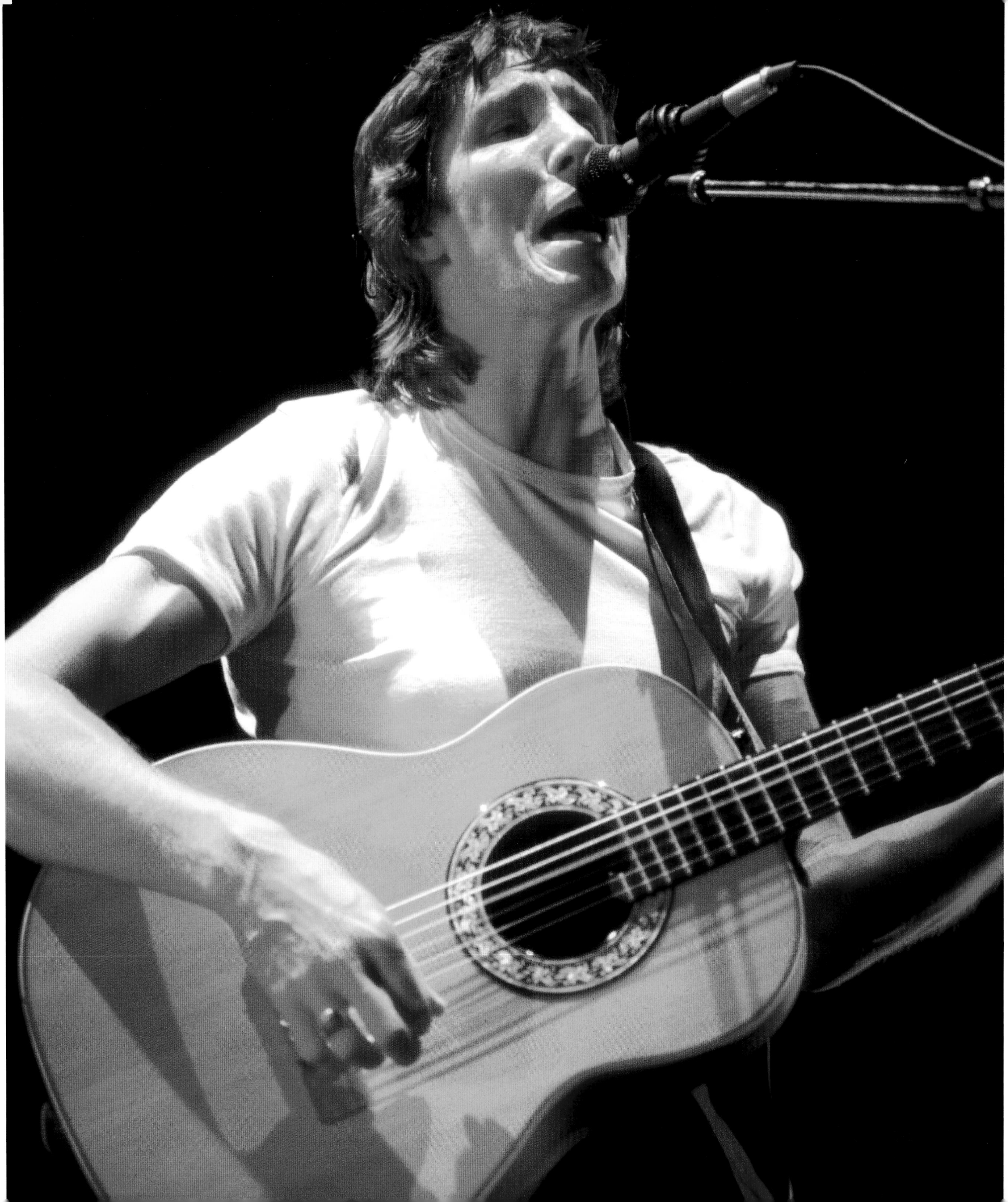

MARCH: *The Final Cut*

Although it was Mason who owned a fleet of classic sports cars, it was Waters who was vengefully speeding around artistic corners on *The Final Cut*. The ghost of his dead father again haunted the emotive, resonant and downright compelling song that was 'The Fletcher Memorial Home' and other lyrics railed at the Conservative government of Margaret Thatcher and the waste of young life in the Falklands War. Waters also drove the other Floyd members out of the studio, stripping Gilmour of production duties and not courting any musical ideas unless they agreed with his own. Session musicians, who would play what they were told, were also drafted in.

MARCH: 'Your Possible Pasts'

The writing appeared to be on the wall for Pink Floyd when, although provisional dates were announced for November 1983, *The Final Cut* did not go out on tour. In fact, the album was a musical coda from *The Wall* project. 'Your Possible Pasts' may have charted strongly as a single in the US in March but one line of Waters' lyrics seemed to be Floydian self-analysis: 'Do you remember? How we used to be?' 'Certainly not recording glorified solo albums under the Floyd banner,' Mason and Gilmour might have retorted. Although Waters had broken new ground with a video EP of some of *The Final Cut* tracks, both he and Gilmour were now working in different studios – on different projects.

JUNE: *Works*

Although they remained with EMI in the UK for their entire career, in America Floyd switched labels from Capitol to CBS Records after *The Dark Side Of The Moon*. To coincide with the release of *The Final Cut* in 1983 Capitol issued *Works*, a compilation of early Floyd material, to cash in. With alternative mixes of well-known tracks, as well as the track 'Embryo', which had, at that time, only appeared on a UK various-artists' compilation, this was an excellent snapshot of Floyd, especially as it contained Waters' 'Several Species Of Small Furry Animals Gathered Together In A Cave And Grooving With A Pict'.

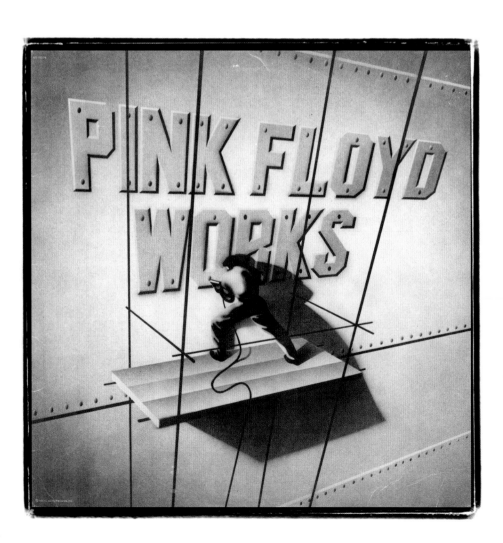

1984

MARCH: Gilmour's *About Face*

When Dave Gilmour began recording his second solo album in France 1983 with Jeff Porcaro (drums), Pino Palladino (bass), Ian Kewley (keyboards) and a host of contributors he appeared to be laying down tracks that would lead him away from the railway station that was Pink Floyd. Musically, *About Face* was slight, fuzzy fun and at times almost too carefree for its own good, although in

retrospect it can be seen that Gilmour was filling up his bucket with creative juices that would be vital when he took on the vacant stationmaster's role at Pink Floyd central in 1986/87.

MARCH – JULY:
Gilmour's *About Face* Tour

Gilmour appeared to cross the post-Floyd Rubicon when he became the first Floyd member to undertake a solo tour when he played 70 dates in the UK, Europe and America between 31 March and 16 July 1984. As well as undertaking a raft of press duties and unfurling his solo material there was also space for the Floyd anthem 'Comfortably Numb' in his well-received sets. A video of his third night at Hammersmith Odeon was subsequently released on video and was transferred to DVD when the earlier format became defunct.

A P R I L: Zee's *Identity*

Dee Harris (left) had been the frontman with Birmingham-based band Fashion whose stripped-down funk cast a 'Love Shadow' over the lower reaches of the UK chart in 1983. He met up with Rick Wright and they got on well enough to collaborate on an album that was released under the name of Zee as *Identity*. Musically, any Floyd fan expecting to hear classic organ drones and melody lines was disappointed as this was, like many an Eighties album, mesmerized by the Fairlight synthesizer and drum sounds that are usually best given a last cigarette before being shot at dawn.

M A Y:

Waters' *The Pros And Cons Of Hitch Hiking*

One wonders how the Pink Floyd saga would have developed in a parallel universe in which Mason and Gilmour opted to work on Waters' *The Pros And Cons Of Hitch Hiking* demos rather than *The Wall*. *Hitch Hiker* became Waters' first proper solo album, although he deployed a similar team to *The Final Cut* including Ray Cooper (percussion), Andy Newmark (drums), Andy Bown (keyboards) and with Michael Kamen writing arrangements for the London Philharmonic Orchestra. Heavyweight artillery was also deployed with David Sanborn playing saxophone and Eric Clapton on guitar. With subject matter revolving around dreams, sex and the mid-life crisis this was heavy and lyrically dense material.

JUNE:

Waters' *The Pros And Cons Of Hitch Hiking* Tour Begins

The most amazing thing about Waters' first *Hitch Hiking* tour of 1984 was that Eric Clapton (right) agreed to play as a sideman. Although the fairly rigid *Hitch Hiker* material and stunning stage presentation were not ideal for 'Slowhand's' subtle wrist, the magic of musical chemistry was in evidence on Floyd favourites like 'Wish You Were Here' and 'Money' where Clapton could lock into the grooves originally laid down by the equally sensitive Gilmour. Clapton left at the end of the first leg of the tour.

1985

JULY: Live Aid

The Live Aid concerts held on 13 July 1985 were one of the greatest musical events of all time. That Bob 'Pink' Geldof was a prime mover meant that David Gilmour received a phone call to get Floyd together to perform. With relations between Gilmour, Waters and Nick Mason approaching legal waters, Gilmour suggested he bring his solo band to play, 'but they

didn't want me'. Gilmour did appear with Bryan Ferry (left), but his guitar could not be heard on the first two songs; his solo on 'Slave To Love' was fantastic, however.

JULY:
Mason's *Profiles*

Away from Pink Floyd, Nick Mason had built up an impressive collection of sports cars and was to establish a company, Ten-Tenths, to hire them out for photoshoots and films to keep them in petrol. Mason also established a company with Rick Fenn, keyboard player for 10cc, to provide music for TV commercials and films. Their 1985 album, *Profiles*, was a neat musical summation of potential instrumental themes and included the single 'Lie For A Lie', featuring lead vocals by Dave Gilmour. 'Even with [Gilmour's] help,' Mason wrote in his memoirs, 'it failed to get close enough to the charts to tarnish the paintwork.'

DECEMBER: Waters Quits

By December 1985 Roger Waters saw his future as a solo artist and believed that Pink Floyd were 'a spent force'. He took steps to dismiss Steve O'Rourke, legally dissolve the group and apportion future royalties. O'Rourke thought it was his duty to inform Gilmour and Mason of Waters' proposals who, after working together on Nick Mason's single 'Lie For A Lie', countered that they intended to carry on trading as Pink Floyd. As the prime creative force behind Floyd's last three albums (*Animals*, *The Wall* and *The Final Cut*) Waters was shocked. 'You'll never f****** get it together to make a record,' he allegedly told Gilmour.

THE GILMOUR-LED ERA: 1986-94

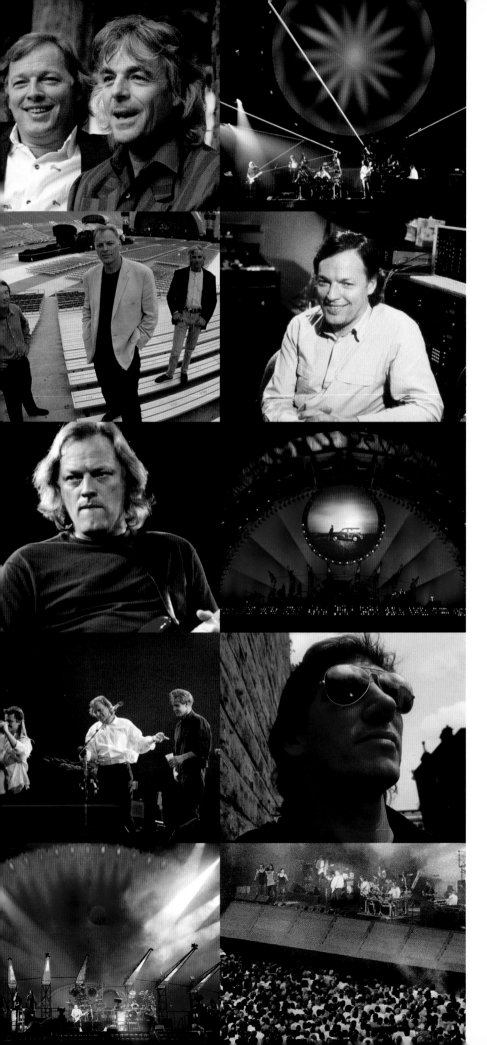

1986-94

Despite legal ammunition being expended by Roger Waters in an effort to cease Pink Floyd operating without him, Dave Gilmour was to lead the band to commercial heights equal to Floyd's mid-1970s peak.

Any worries about the strength of new Pink Floyd material undiluted by Waters was unfounded when *A Momentary Lapse Of Reason* (1987) topped the charts on both sides of the Atlantic and the band learned to fly through video with the young MTV generation. As far as live shows went the *A Momentary Lapse Of Reason* and *Division Bell* tours would be Floyd's most lucrative ever, bringing home bacon worth in excess of $300 million. Waters' inflatable pig – adjusted for legal reasons – was to become a trademark. With Nick Mason and Rick Wright augmented by session musicians in the studio and on the road classic material had never been so forensically played, although to some original fans it was like double-glazing replacing original wooden windows.

As a solo artist, Waters was to record and tour striking and ambitious concept pieces like *Radio K.A.O.S.* (1987); when the wall was taken down in Berlin, he rebuilt his own in its place with a stunning reenactment of his most famous musical piece. Waters would also perform classic Floyd material live and, although there was some verbal tennis in the press, the Floyd legacy was being preserved and curated by both parties. Pink Floyd albums transferred onto CD sold by the bucket load to old and new fans alike.

1986

FEBRUARY: Wright Returns

Since working for a salary on *The Wall* tour and his Zee collaboration, Rick Wright had retired to the wings of the music business to enjoy life with his new wife and homes in the Greek islands. He did contact Gilmour when the guitarist was in Greece in the summer of 1985 offering his services for any new Gilmour project. In fact Gilmour had already begun to lay down material with producer Bob Ezrin and had been assisted on lyrics by former Slapp Happy and Henry Cow singer Anthony Moore. Gilmour later asked Wright to contribute to the sessions.

NOVEMBER: Press Release

'Pink Floyd is alive, well and recording in England,' EMI announced proudly in a press release on 11 November 1986. In fact, despite Mason and Wright being on board – literally, with the recording sessions taking place on Gilmour's houseboat studio – the majority of this material mostly written by Gilmour, was being recorded by session musicians including bass player Tony Levin, and drummers Carmine Appice and Jim Keltner. But for EMI, Gilmour and a legion of fans around the world the thought that *The Final Cut* was not the end was exciting indeed.

1987

APRIL: Waters Declares Legal Action

Roger Waters had got wind of Gilmour's intentions well in advance of the EMI press release and in October 1986 had taken matters to the High Court. Even though Waters had offered the name to Mason and Gilmour in 1985 when unofficially leaving, he did not believe that they would actually dare to record without him. Although a game of legal tennis ensued, with both parties giving their side to the press, the bottom line was that Waters could not stop Mason and Gilmour – with Wright on salary – releasing 'new' Pink Floyd material.

JUNE:

Waters' *Radio K.A.O.S.*

Roger Waters released his second solo album, *Radio K.A.O.S.*, in June 1987. This was a concept album about a disabled young Welshman whose special mental powers allow him to hack into military computers and pretend to start – and then avert – a Third World War. Like the ending of *The Watchmen* graphic novel (1986/87) this fake threat to humanity is intended to unite the world, although Waters' political convictions took a swipe at Margaret Thatcher, Ronald Reagan, the plight of UK miners (a male-voice choir feature on 'The Tide Is Turning') and the rigid formatting of American FM radio stations. Musically, the

album was smeared with Eighties' technology, from a Fairlight synthesizer to computerized voices, and sold – for a Floyd-related album – poorly.

AUGUST-NOVEMBER:
Waters' *Radio K.A.O.S.* Tour

Roger Waters took *Radio K.A.O.S.* out on the road in 1987 for a 37-date tour that was confined to North America, apart from two final dates in Wembley, England. Backed by his 'Bleeding Hearts' tour band the staging was lavish and, in keeping with the *Radio K.A.O.S.* theme, featured a radio DJ talking between songs, introducing original footage of 'Arnold Layne' as well as allowing lucky fans to talk to Waters through a telephone box in the auditorium at each venue. Did anyone dare to ask, 'When are Floyd getting back together?'? As well as *Radio K.A.O.S.* material, Waters served up a number of Floyd classics including 'Money', 'Breathe', 'Welcome To The Machine' and 'Wish You Were Here'.

SEPTEMBER:
A Momentary Lapse Of Reason

That the new Pink Floyd album was called *A Momentary Lapse Of Reason* (1987) probably summed up Waters' feeling about the mental state of his former band-mates. With Storm Thorgerson's arresting cover art featuring an endless river of beds it certainly looked like a Floyd album. 'Learning To Fly' was the outstanding track, in which Gilmour, in some respects after being overshadowed by Waters' songwriting and production dominance, demonstrated that he was now learning to 'create' again. That the album reached No. 1 in the UK and America showed that there were plenty of Floyd fans, old and new, willing continue the journey.

PINK FLOYD

A Momentary Lapse of Reason

SEPTEMBER - DECEMBER:

A Momentary Lapse Of Reason Tour

The *A Momentary Lapse Of Reason* tour of North America kicked off in Lansdowne Park, Ottowa, Canada on 9 September and by Christmas the band had completed over 50 dates. Gilmour, Mason and Wright were augmented by Tim Renwick (guitar), Jon Carin (synthesizers), Guy Pratt (bass), Gary Wallis (percussion) and – eventually – three backing singers. Although the new album was the centerpiece, audiences enjoyed old classics like 'Money', 'Another Brick In The Wall' and 'Comfortably Numb'. The staging included high-tech visual effects, although to circumnavigate legal action Waters' 'trademark' inflatable pig was augmented by two large testicles.

SEPTEMBER - JUNE 1988:

Singles Released

Pink Floyd promoted the new album hard with Gilmour and Mason conducting a large number of charming telephone interviews with the music press, and three singles would be culled from the album. 'Learning To Fly' fast became a Floyd classic and the obligatory video featured the band intercut with images of hang-gliders and an American-Indian boy who learns to soar like an eagle. This won an MTV Best Concept video award in 1988 beating XTC, INXS, U2 and George Harrison who were also shortlisted. 'On The Turning Away' and 'One Slip' were less potent single material but released anyway.

DECEMBER:

Gilmour/Waters' Dispute Settled

Roger Waters had remained a shareholder in Pink Floyd. He had done his best to block the release of *A Momentary Lapse Of Reason* and subsequent tour under the name Pink Floyd to the extent that Floyd's road crew for the tour included lawyers to fight any threat of legal action. Matters were finally resolved between Waters and Gilmour during a face-to-face meeting on Gilmour's houseboat on 23 December 1987. The meeting resulted in a legal document that would allow Gilmour and Mason to retain the Pink Floyd name 'in perpetuity' in return for Waters being allowed some form of royalties, as well as control over *The Wall*.

NESTOR schoonmakers

45   16   11   30.25
ENTER GATE 3   ADULT
MOLSON CANADIAN ROCKS
Q107 PRESENTS PINK FLOYD
COCA-COLA CLASSIC
CNE STADIUM/RAIN OR SHINE
NO CAMERAS OR RECORDERS
FRI MAY 13 1988 8 PM

1988

JANUARY: World Tour '88 Begins

Although the *A Momentary Lapse Of Reason* tour was to be one of the most financially successful of the Eighties, Nick Mason revealed in his autobiography *Inside Out* (2004) that the seed capital to finance the employment of musicians, road crew, set, light and cinematic construction came from Dave Gilmour and himself. Potential backers would have, at this stage, been made nervous by Waters' legal threats against the tour. Mason raised his half by selling 'my most prized possession, and an old family friend': a rare classic 1962 GTO Ferrari, and 'had little trouble in financing my half of the tour set-up costs'. By the time of the World Tour that took up most of 1988 the band were well into profit.

JANUARY:

Inflatable Bed Promo

The *A Momentary Lapse Of Reason* world tour was promoted with a rather unique photo opportunity for journalists. A giant inflatable of one of the beds photographed by Storm Thorgerson for the album cover shoot was manufactured, filled with helium and on 28 January 1988 was floated down the River Thames in front of the Houses of Parliament. Gilmour, Mason and Wright were not present as they were already playing the third date of the tour in Sydney, Australia, on that day.

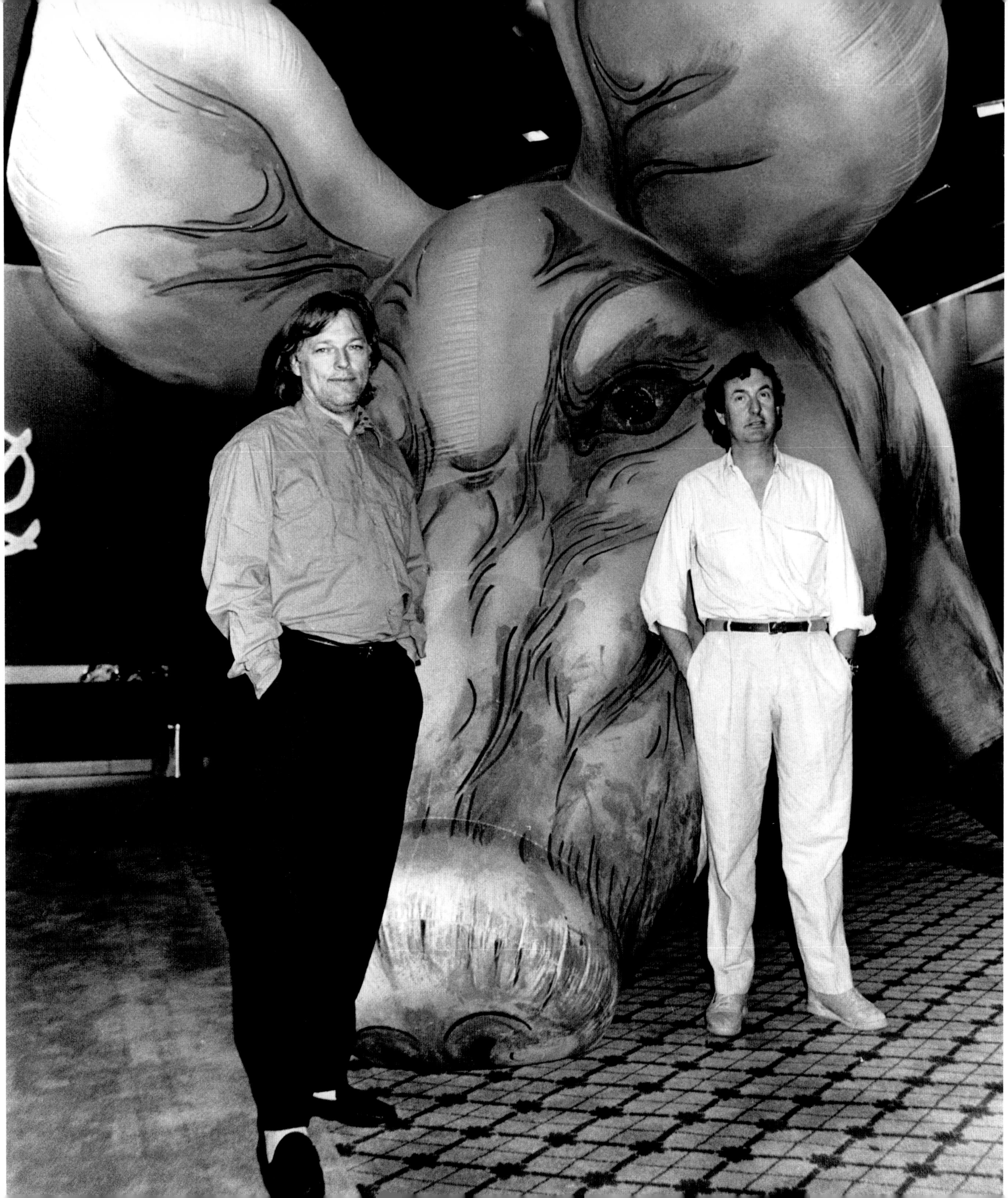

NOVEMBER:

Delicate Sound Of Thunder

Released on 22 November 1988

Delicate Sound Of Thunder captured a fully road-tested, Gilmour-led Pink Floyd. The band were recorded over five nights at the Nassau Coliseum, New York, and the best tracks were selected from this material, although elements of some were slightly tweaked at Abbey Road Studios. This hardly mattered to Floyd fans who, along with the latest album, were treated to a selection of classic material including 'Shine On You Crazy Diamond', 'Money', 'Wish You Were Here' and 'Time', all sung by Gilmour. The album peaked at No. 11 in both the US and UK charts.

1989
MAY–JULY:

Another Lapse Tour

The final leg of what had turned into three years of touring *A Momentary Lapse Of Reason* took place in Europe between May and July 1989. Shows were slick and Pink Floyd even performed in Moscow where their equipment was flown in and out on Russian military cargo planes. Nick Mason reported that the band were able to visit Monino, the Russian air force museum which, at that time, hardly anyone outside of the Soviet Union had been allowed to see. Appropriately, *Delicate Sound Of Thunder* was the first rock album to played in space: it had taken off with the Soviet cosmonauts aboard Soyuz TM-7 the previous November!

JULY:
Controversy In Venice

One of the final performances of the spectacular *Another Lapse* tour was in a suitably spectacular location: Venice. Floyd performed on a moored barge on the Grand Canal in front of St Mark's Square. Broadcast by satellite and held in such a perfect setting, this concert was a fantastic success allowing the band to see waves of water as well as waves of fans from the stage. Behind-the-scenes wrangling had been typically Italian, with gondoliers demanding money not to blow their whistles during the performance. Despite Pink Floyd's reassurances to the contrary, the 200,000 fans present and the noise from the concert itself allegedly caused some damage to buildings and bridges.

1990
JUNE:
Knebworth Festival

Pink Floyd had been the first major band to commit to playing the 1990 Knebworth Festival and in doing so secured top-billing over Paul McCartney. Their entrance was delayed by McCartney playing numerous encores and, due to high winds, the Floyd road crew had to take down the band's large circular screen for safety reasons. Despite this, Floyd ended up closing the show to an audience who enjoyed the performance despite drizzling rain. A young Candy Dulfer was part of the touring band for this performance playing a memorable saxophone solo on 'Shine On You Crazy Diamond'. Released later in 1990 her debut album *Saxuality* sold a million copies.

JULY:
Waters Performs *The Wall* In Berlin

Roger Waters once joked that he would only perform *The Wall* again if the Berlin Wall came down. This miracle officially happened in 1990, contributing to the end of the Cold War. Waters was approached to re-stage *The Wall* for the charity Memorial Fund for Disaster Relief. Logistically, this was probably the most ambitious Floyd-related performance ever with the 'new' Berlin Wall and attendant projections, lights and inflatables costing in the region of £4 million. Backed by his current touring band Waters deployed a number of special guests like The Scorpions, Sinéad O'Connor, Van Morrison and actor Tim Curry. 250,000 were in attendance.

1991
OCTOBER: La Carrera Panamericana

'As far as Pink Floyd was concerned the 1990s nearly didn't happen,' wrote Nick Mason in his autobiography *Inside Out*. This was not due to legal feuding but that Dave Gilmour and manager Steve O'Rourke were nearly killed when racing in the Carrera Panamericana along the length of Mexico. Their C-type Jaguar had gone over the edge of a cliff at 130 kph (80 mph) and although Gilmour escaped with cuts and bruises, O'Rourke suffered a fractured leg. Nick Mason, who had participated in the race with O'Rourke two years earlier, went on to finish in the first 10 in his own C-type Jag. A film of the race, *La Carrera Panamericana*, was released in 1992 with a soundtrack entirely by Pink Floyd.

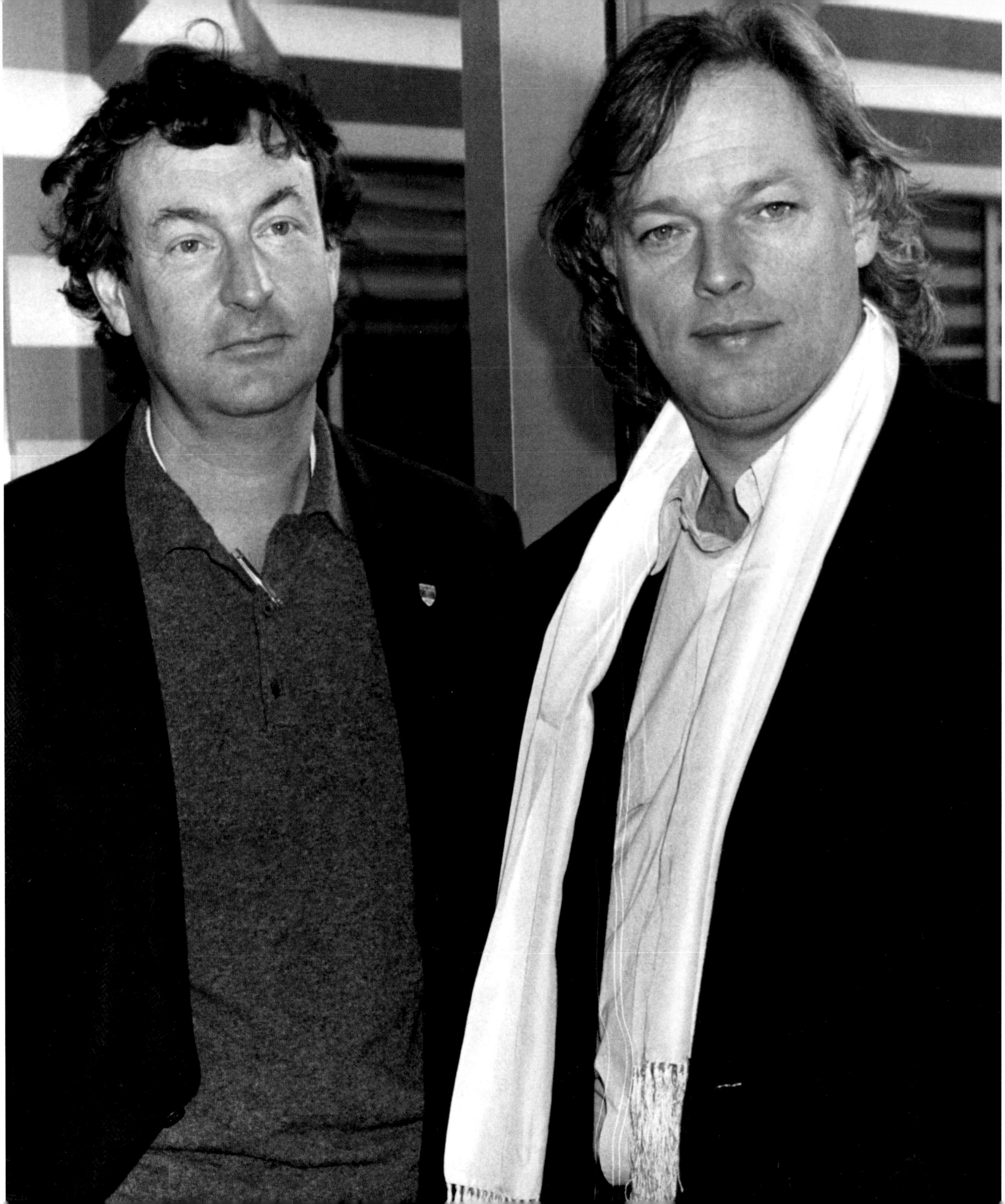

1992

APRIL: Ivor Novello Award

Although the Gilmour-led Floyd and Roger Waters' solo career were both firing on all cylinders, due to their longevity the Nineties saw Pink Floyd begin to accumulate a number of awards. In April 1992 the band received a well-deserved Ivor Novello Award for their outstanding contribution to British music. As the Novello Awards celebrate British songwriters this was recognition of the strength, vitality and appeal of the music written and performed by Waters, Gilmour, Wright and Mason.

SEPTEMBER:

Waters' *Amused To Death*

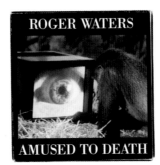

'What is the shelf-life of a teenage queen?' asked Roger Waters on the title track of his latest album *Amused To Death*. Waters explained in one interview that the album, 'explores the idea of television as medicine: it's either healing us or killing us. The truth is it's doing both, healing us as a target audience but killing off our respective cultures.' Musically, the album was more coherent and aurally potent than the overblown *K.A.O.S.* concept. Waters incorporated his own strong convictions in the lyrics, as well as including a backwards recorded message to Stanley Kubrick who refused permission to use a sample from the HAL computer from the *2001: A Space Odyssey* movie. What promised to be a perfect vehicle for multimedia performance was not toured, even though the album reached the UK Top 10.

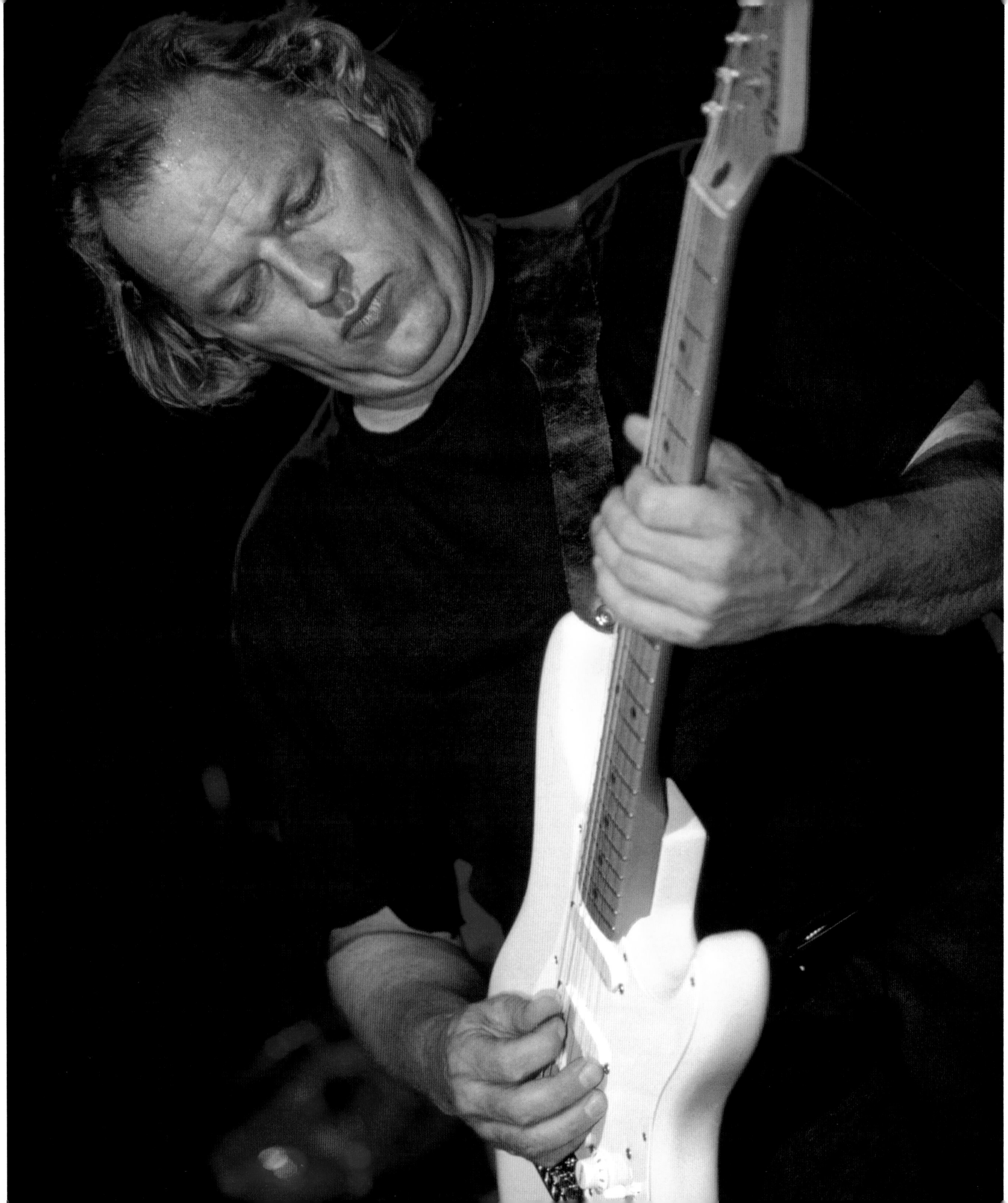

NOVEMBER:

Shine On

Pink Floyd's 25th anniversary was celebrated by EMI with a nine-CD box set entitled *Shine On* containing selected albums from their discography. These were: *A Saucerful Of Secrets*; *Meddle*; *The Dark Side Of The Moon*; *Wish You Were Here*; *Animals*; *The Wall* (double album); and *A Momentary Lapse Of Reason*. There was a bonus CD that included their first five singles, documenting the transition from Barrett's leadership to the more democratic direction taken after his departure; Richard Wright took the lead vocal on fourth single 'It Would Be So Nice'. Many Floyd fans wondered why *Ummagumma* and Floyd's soundtrack work were not included.

1994

MARCH:

The Division Bell

In 1993 Gilmour, Mason and Wright got back to basics during early sessions for their next album by writing and recording alone. They only brought in additional musicians, like Guy Pratt, when they had a number of ideas to work into songs. Lyrically, Gilmour was assisted by his new girlfriend (and future second wife), Polly Samson. When the band had trouble coming up with a title for the new album, they turned to author (and friend of Gilmour) Douglas Adams, who suggested 'The Division Bell', which was a lyric from the song 'High Hopes'. Released in March, the album, with its clean modern sound, topped the charts in the UK and the USA.

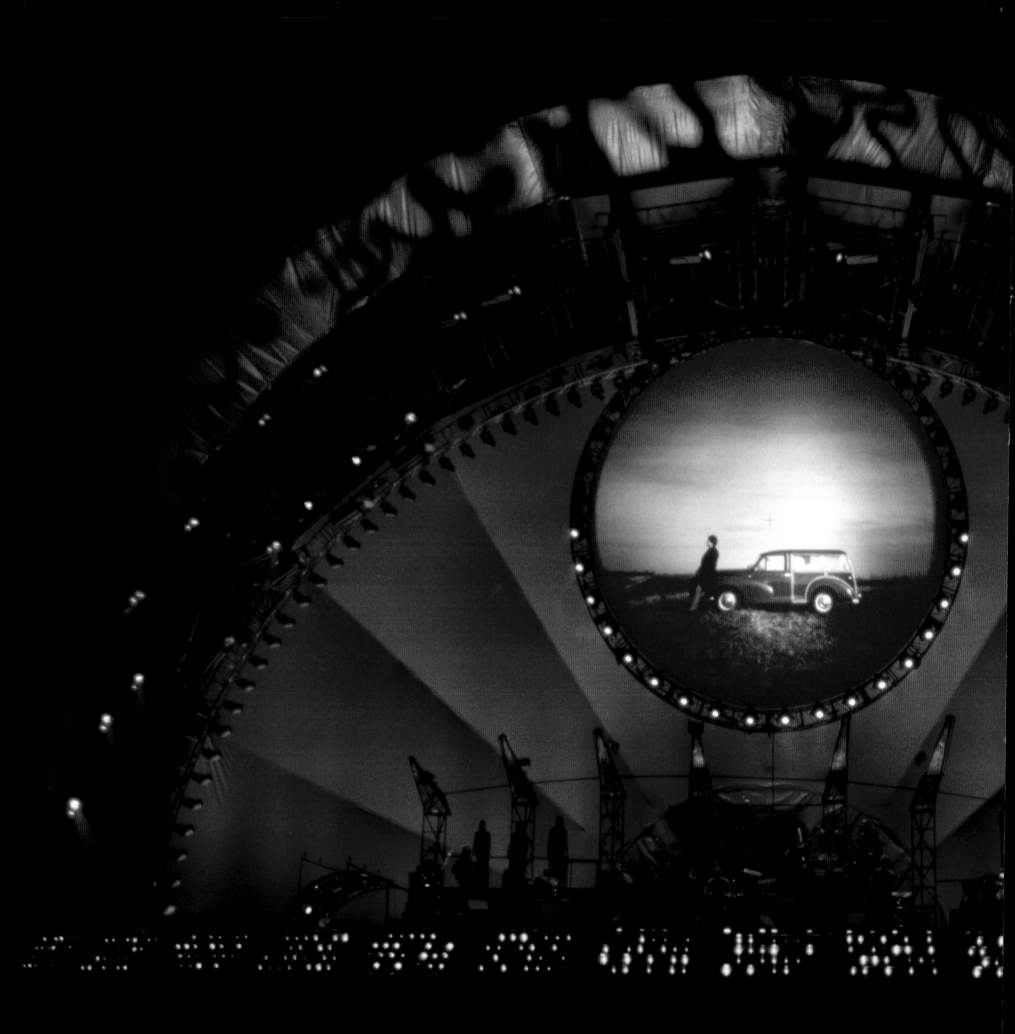

MARCH—OCTOBER:
The Division Bell Tour

The Division Bell tour was sponsored in part by Volkswagen which allowed the band to finance the construction of a mammoth touring beast that included three stages, two Boeing 747 cargo planes and a road crew of around 200. The most impressive stage props were two Skyship 600 airships – one for America and one for Europe – and a vast mirror-ball. Dick Parry (saxophone), Gary Wallis (percussion), Guy Pratt (bass), Jon Carin (keyboards) and Tim Renwick (guitar) and three backing singers were on hand when the World Tour kicked off in Miami on 29 March 1994. By the time it finished in October the tour had grossed an estimated £150 million.

MAY– OCTOBER:

Singles Released

Despite Roger Waters' caustic comment to one journalist: 'Lyrics written by the new wife? I mean, give me a break!', *The Division Bell* sounded like Pink Floyd wrapped in Eighties' studio technology, but did contain strong single material. Both 'Take It Back' and the anthemic 'High Hopes' made the UK Top 30 in 1994. One of the strongest tracks on the album was Richard Wright's 'Wearing The Inside Out', which was his first lead vocal

in over 20 years. Wright had his full-time, band-member-status privileges returned and made a full contribution in the studio and on the road.

OCTOBER:

Earl's Court Residency

The Division Bell tour ended with residency at Earl's Court in London with all proceeds being given to a large number of charities. Although the first night had to be re-scheduled after about 30 seconds due to a seating collapse, the well-oiled live Floyd machine delighted audiences with a multimedia music extravaganza that paid full tribute to their past including now-iconic songs like 'Astronomy Domine', 'Shine On You Crazy Diamond' and 'Wish You Were Here'. Douglas Adams was given the ultimate birthday present on 28 October by being allowed to strum a guitar on stage during 'Brain Damage'.

NOVEMBER:

Official End Of Pink Floyd

By leading Pink Floyd through two albums and their most financially successful tours Dave Gilmour had shown that there was life after Roger Waters. Although not known at the time *The Division Bell* was the final album and tour under the Pink Floyd banner. Although Nick Mason hoped that there might be another album and spoke in his autobiography of 'a twist on the unplugged concept', as leader and main creative force Gilmour was more interested in being a family man. Pink Floyd would never reconvene for a new studio album and, despite two pulse-racing moments, never played live again.

BEYOND PINK FLOYD: 1995—PRESENT

1995-PRESENT

The last album of new Pink Floyd material was released in 1994, but the subsequent years were to highlight the band's legendary status. Although Waters, Gilmour, Mason and Wright would throw out solo albums and Gilmour and Waters would tour occasionally, the sheer power and size of the Floyd musical glacier would continually move forward to add fans to the millions worldwide who adored the band.

Awards, anniversaries and inductions into the UK and US Music Halls Of Fame were tangible rewards although reissues of albums, unearthing of rare archive footage or Waters restaging *The Dark Side Of The Moon* excited most. The thought of the cold war between Waters and Gilmour ending in reunion was a constant speculation and was a question posed during every promotional interview whether to discuss the band's legacy, *The Wall* or the publication of Nick Mason's memoirs.

When Waters, Gilmour, Wright and Mason did reconvene for Live 8 in 2005 this proved to be a one-off performance. The opportunity to play again when Syd Barrett's death was commemorated in a 2007 concert was missed when Waters did not appear on stage with Gilmour, Wright and Mason to play 'Arnold Layne'. In death Barrett's legacy as a songwriting genius and the creative force in the early Pink Floyd was acknowledged by his fellow band members and a new generation of fans and bands. The death of Richard Wright in 2008 confirmed that Live 8 had been the last performance by the classic Pink Floyd line-up.

1995

MARCH: Grammy Award

Although *The Division Bell* was the last new album and tour vehicle for Pink Floyd there was an unexpected coda in March 1995 when the track 'Marooned' won a Grammy for Best Rock Instrumental Performance. Over a relaxed rhythm and sound effects of floating seagulls and even whale-song Gilmour had unfurled one of his finest, most-sensitive and most-compelling guitar solos. Romantic and sensual were not normally words associated with Pink Floyd tracks but 'Marooned' ticked both boxes and was often rotated on radio at the Champagne end of the dinner jazz wavelength. 'Marooned' was co-written by Wright.

JUNE: *P*U*L*S*E*

Although the unique flashing LED packaging for the two-CD issue received a lot of attention (and made it easier to find in record shops) *P*U*L*S*E* was a compelling document of *The Division Bell* tour. Notable for including a complete performance of *The Dark Side Of The Moon* and a modern prowl through the crowd-pleasing resurrection of 'Astronomy Domine' it also showcased the precision of Gilmour, Mason, Wright and the backing musicians of the touring unit Pink Floyd Mark III. Floyd fans were frustrated that the 22-minute 'Soundscape' (one of the ambient experiments from *The Division Bell* sessions) was only on the *cassette* version.

1996

SEPTEMBER:
London '66–'67 EP

Released in September 1995 the *London '66-'67* EP was the most significant Pink Floyd release since *The Wall*. Hardcore fans could finally and officially hear the full-length version of 'Interstellar Overdrive' recorded by Joe Boyd that had tantalized ears for only three minutes in *Tonite Let's All Make Love In London* (1968). The other track was a jam of 'Nick's Boogie'. Musically this was Floyd at their most pioneering with Syd Barrett's guitar spraying jarring and timepiece texture across a beautiful landscape created by Waters' melodic bass, Mason's drumming and Rick Wright's delicious Farfisa organ runs. Released on DVD in 2005 Floyd fans could also watch assembled footage of this timewarp.

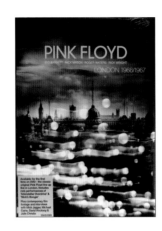

JANUARY:
Rock And Roll Hall Of Fame

Although Pink Floyd were not defending their heavyweight title in the ring anymore, they were no longer anonymous figures and enjoyed all the personal trappings of being one of the world's most successful and influential bands. On 17 January 1996 at the Waldorf-Astoria Hotel in New York Gilmour, Wright and Mason were inducted into The Rock And Roll Hall Of Fame by Smashing Pumpkins frontman Billy Corgan (right). After receiving the award Nick Mason returned to his seat, whilst Gilmour, Corgan and Wright performed an acoustic version of 'Wish You Were Here' (which may have been directed at Roger Waters).

Pink Floyd ✤ London ✤ '66–'67

TAKEN FROM THE FILM BY PETER WHITEHEAD

INCLUDES THE 'DEFINITIVE' VERSION OF 'INTERSTELLAR OVERDRIVE'

BOOKLET CONTAINS UNIQUE STILLS FROM THE RECORDING SESSION

Syd Barrett ✤ Nick Mason
Roger Waters ✤ Rick Wright

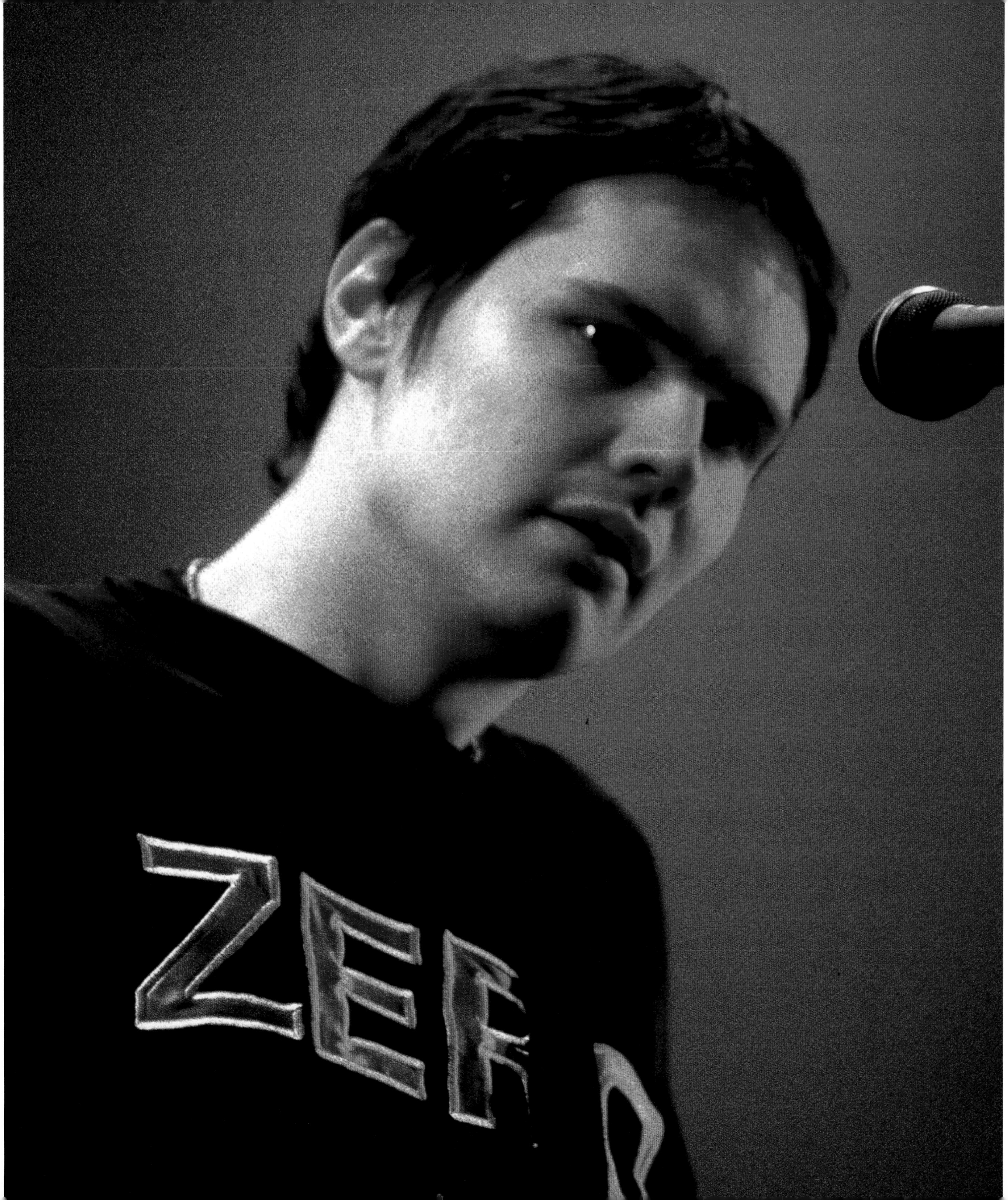
ZER

JUNE:

Gilmour Plays On *Quadrophenia*

On 29 June 1996 Pete Townshend (above, right) staged the first full live performance of his 1973 rock opera *Quadrophenia* for the Prince's Trust charity at London's Hyde Park in front of an estimated 150,000 people. An all-star cast featured Phil Daniels as the narrator, Gary Glitter as the rocker, Trevor McDonald as the newsreader and Dave Gilmour as the bus driver. Gilmour played guitar and shared vocal duties on 'The Dirty Jobs' and wore for the first – and possibly the last – time a pair of braces on stage. Apart from that, this was a busman's holiday indeed!

OCTOBER: Wright's *Broken China*

In October 1996 Richard Wright released a very personal solo album. Although the name was lyrically coded, *Broken China* explored the depression suffered by his third wife, Mildred. 'I wanted to express my feelings about what I was seeing,' he told an interviewer at the time. Musically, the sound of the album contained elements of the ambient Floyd sound and

Wright was assisted by an impressive list of collaborators including Floyd touring guitarists Tim Renwick and Dominic Miller, drummer Manu Katche and bass player Pino Palladino. Sinéad O'Connor featured as guest lead vocalist on two tracks, 'Reaching For The Rail' and 'Breakthrough'.

1999

JULY:

Waters' *In The Flesh* Tours Begin

In July 1999 Roger Waters commenced his first major tour since promoting *Radio K.A.O.S.* in 1987. Playing to enthusiastic crowds Waters delivered a set that carefully balanced the Floyd legacy with his own solo work. The band were drilled to perfection and included famed Sixties singer P.P. Arnold on vocals as well as the usual suspects: Andy Fairweather-Low (guitar), Snowy White (guitar) and Doyle Bramhall II (keyboards). The tour was confined to America for a month of dates in 1999 and 2000; in 2002 Waters went global, taking the tour from South Africa to Japan, and ending up at Glastonbury on 30 June 2002.

2000

MARCH:

Is There Anybody Out There? The Wall Live 1980–81

The twentieth anniversary of *The Wall* was not only celebrated with a DVD release featuring a delicious commentary from Waters, director Alan Parker and artist Gerald Scarfe but a live album pieced together from 16 hours of music recorded during the Earl's Court performances. *Is There Anybody Out There? The Wall Live 1980–81* captured the band ploughing through Waters' creation at full steam and the sheer power and punch of the music was as arresting as the visual spectacle of the concerts. The band re-formed to promote the album; sadly this was only individually in front of journalists' dictaphones.

DECEMBER: Waters' *In The Flesh*

Initially Roger Waters' record company wanted the live album of *In The Flesh* to be a single CD. He convinced them otherwise and the resulting two-CD release presented Floyd fans with the entire two-hour set. Drawn from performances in Phoenix, Las Vegas, Irvine and Portland during the second tour in 2000 this was essentially Floyd and Waters' greatest hits from 'Set The Controls To The Heart Of The Sun' to a new song 'Each Small Candle' that dealt with small acts of humanity during war. Waters' fans also saw him *In The Flesh* on the DVD release of the Portland show.

2001

JUNE:

The Meltdown Festival

When Robert Wyatt was asked to curate the Meltdown Festival at the Royal Festival Hall, London, in June 2001 an eclectic mix of artists was guaranteed. The surprise package was Dave Gilmour agreeing to play in a venue that only seated 2,000 people with no room for airships and inflatables. Concentrating on the music Gilmour opened the set alone with an acoustic guitar and 'Shine On You Crazy Diamond'. Joined by a hand-picked band and nine backing singers Gilmour then prowled through undergrowth as neglected as 'Fat Old Sun' from *Atom Heart Mother* to the well-trimmed lawn of 'Wish You Were Here'. The final encore was a real shock: 'Hushabye Mountain' from the film *Chitty Chitty Bang Bang* (1968). The entire concert was captured for posterity and released on DVD in October 2002 as *David Gilmour In Concert*.

DAVID GILMOUR

FRP Free Range Pigs   FRP-CDR/009

GILMOUR'S MELTDOWN 2001

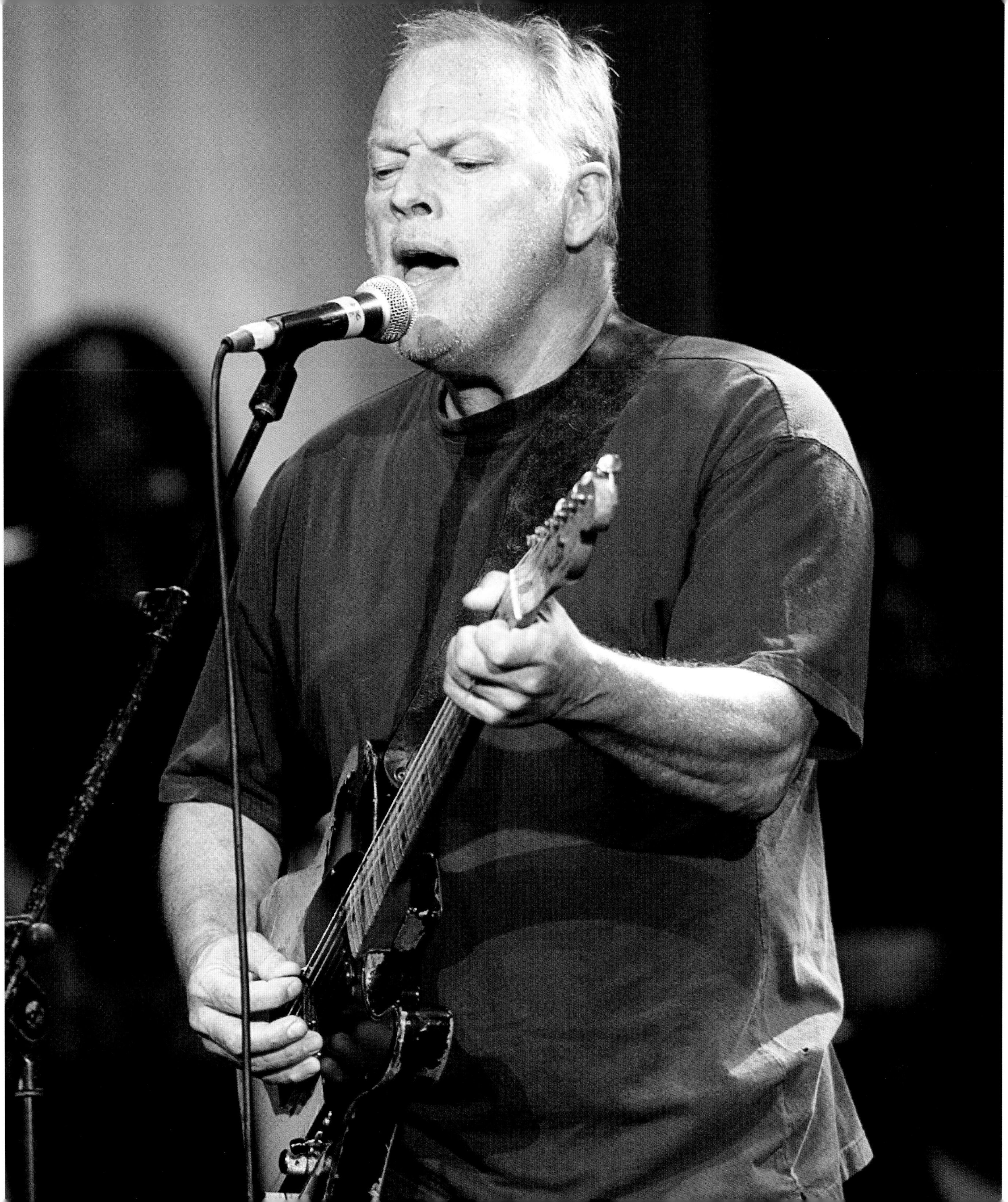

NOVEMBER:

Echoes: The Best Of Pink Floyd

Floyd had been ill-served by compilation albums: *Relics* and *A Collection Of Great Dance Songs* were poorly cobbled shoes. This all changed in November 2001 with the release of the career-spanning *Echoes: The Best Of Pink Floyd*. What made this 26-track, two-CD set work was the fact that the running order was not chronological but tracks from all different eras and line-ups sat comfortably next to or segued into each other. The classic 1967 single 'See Emily Play' was followed by 'The Happiest Days of Our Lives' and then 'Another Brick In The Wall (Part 2)' from *The Wall* (both 1979). Nick Mason revealed in his autobiography that the band had a major say in the compilation,

devising a voting system for inclusion; Roger Waters, he said, 'would only vote for his own tracks'.

PINK FLOYD ☉ BACK CATALOGUE

NOVEMBER: BBC Omnibus

Prior to the broadband explosion it was hard to see archive footage of the early Floyd. This was remedied on 24 November 2001 when the BBC Omnibus programme aired a one-hour documentary entitled *The Pink Floyd And Syd Barrett Story*. The focus was on Barrett and, although Waters and early

associates like guitarist Bob Klose, photographer Mick Rock and even Blur guitarist Graham Coxon were interviewed, the arresting archive footage and pictures of the Barrett-led Floyd performing tracks like 'Interstellar Overdrive' made for compelling viewing. 'Too loud,' Barrett apparently told his mother after watching the TV broadcast at his Cambridge home.

2003

OCTOBER: Steve O'Rourke Dies

The first member of Pink Floyd passed away on 30 October 2003 when manager Steve O'Rourke died in Miami of a stroke aged 63. The butt of early cruel verbal jokes (Waters once called him a 'glorified booker') he was the indefatigable engineer ensuring that the Floyd engine ran smoothly, organizing everything from tour finances to the ordering of concert airships. A fanatical motor-racing enthusiast, one of his career highlights was finishing 11th in the Le Mans 24-hour race in 1985. At his funeral service held in Chichester Cathedral on 14 November Mason, Wright and Gilmour paid tribute to him, performing 'Fat Old Sun' and – appropriately – 'The Great Gig In The Sky'.

NOVEMBER:
Gilmour Awarded CBE

In November 2003 David Gilmour had the rare pleasure of meeting the Queen at Buckingham Palace to receive a CBE for his services to music. That he had also undertaken a number of charity-based projects (including donating the proceeds – £3.6 million – of the sale of a house to Crisis) must have also been a factor in receiving this honour. According to Gilmour, when he received his honour from the Queen she said, '"Pink Floyd have been doing well for a long time", and I had to agree.' Gilmour attended the ceremony with his wife Polly, daughter Alice and son Charlie.

2004
SEPTEMBER:
The Strat Pack Concert

Throughout his career, the Fender Stratocaster was David Gilmour's guitar of choice and he had always been comfortable to discuss his taste in plank-spanking equipment ever since joining the band. On 24 September 2004 he helped celebrate the 50th anniversary of the Fender guitar by participating in a charity concert at Wembley. Gilmour used the million-dollar Strat No. 0001 (which he owned) to perform 'Marooned' and 'Coming Back To Life' and reverted to his famed 1957 reissue for the final track 'Sorrow'. Other performers included Johnny Marr of Smiths fame, Joe Walsh from the Eagles and Amy Winehouse!

THE
STRAT PACK
LIVE IN CONCERT
JOE WALSH
DAVID GILMOUR
BRIAN MAY
PAUL RODGERS
RONNIE WOOD
HANK MARVIN
THE CRICKETS
ALBERT LEE
GARY MOORE
MIKE RUTHERFORD
PAUL CARRACK
PHIL MANZANERA
AMY WINEHOUSE
JAMIE CULLUM
THERESA ANDERSSON
DVD
CELEBRATING 50 YEARS OF THE FENDER STRATOCASTER

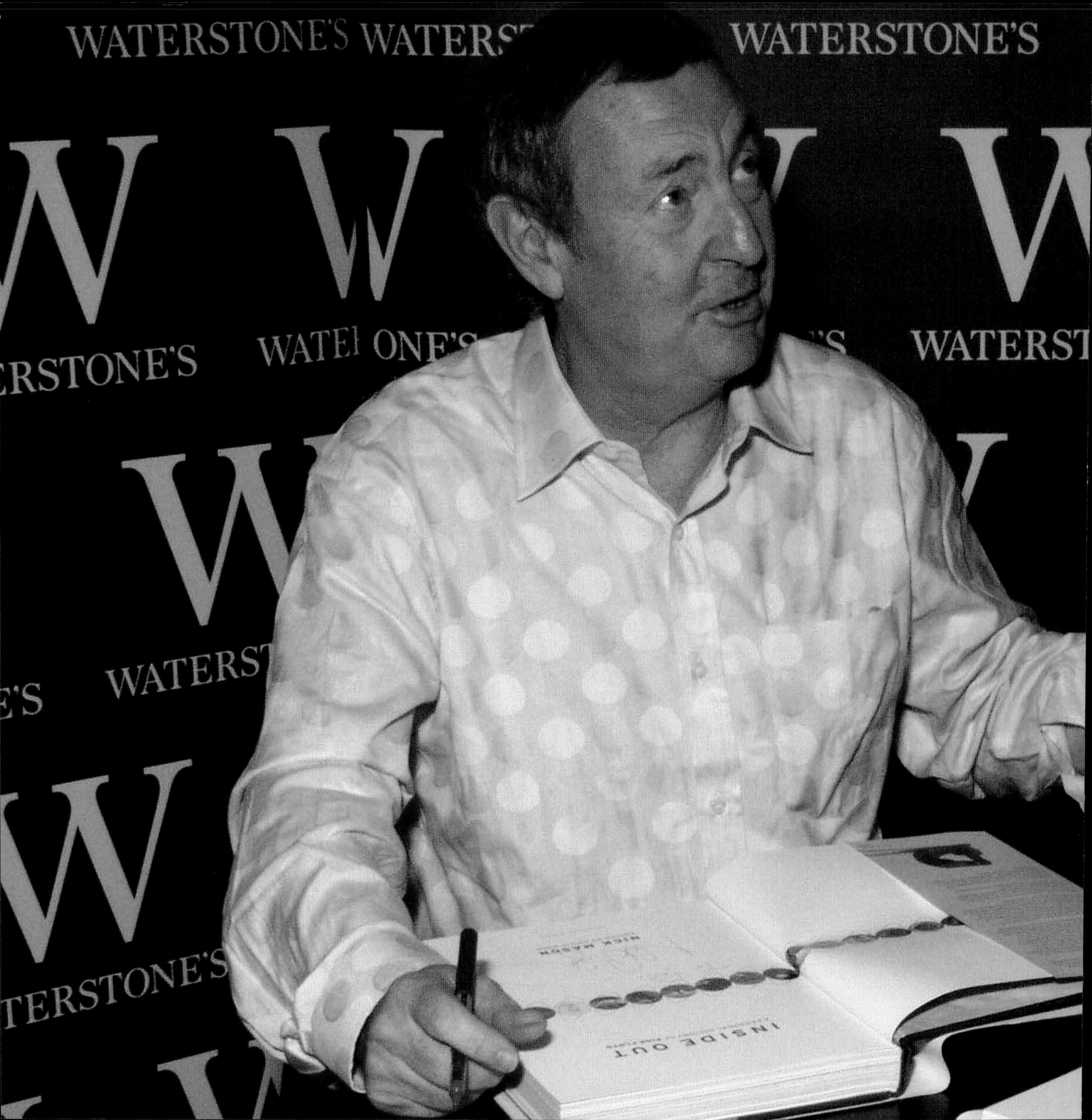
WATERSTONE'S
WATERSTONE'S
INSIDE OUT
NICK MASON

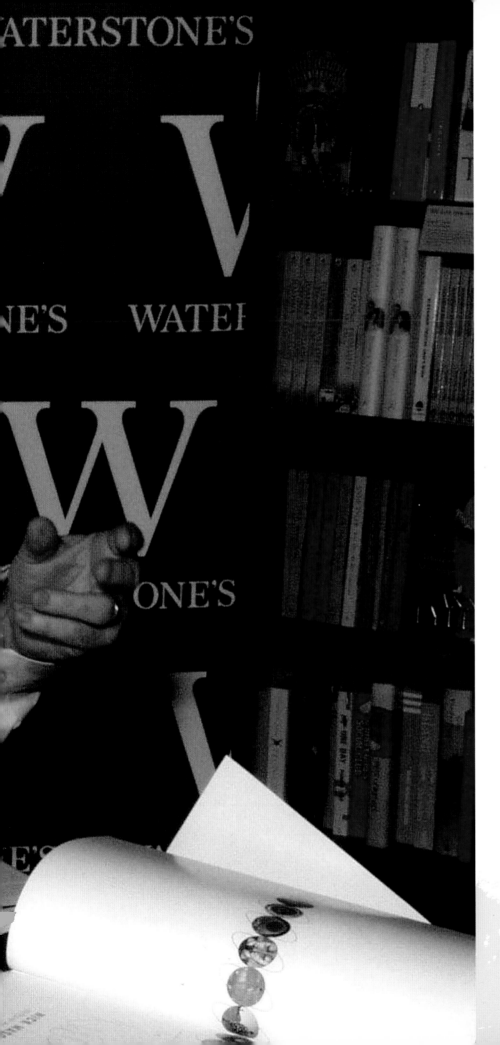

OCTOBER:

Mason's *Inside Out:* *A Personal History Of Pink Floyd*

In 2004 Nick Mason published his personal history of Pink Floyd: *Inside Out*. Like the author it was too well-mannered to contain any sordid revelations but gave a wry insight into the inner workings of the Floyd machine. This ranged from a first meeting at college where Mason refused to lend Waters his unreliable Austin Seven, to Bill Graham arranging a pen full of pigs backstage when Floyd were touring *Animals*. The best 'revelation' was that EMI had presented Mason – and we

assume the rest of Floyd – with a gold Rolex watch in 1977 to commemorate 10 years of service.

2005

JULY: Live 8

The most amazing thing about Floyd's brief four-song reunion for Bob 'Pink' Geldof's Live 8 concert was the group hug. That it was initiated by Waters as the band prepared to walk off stage shows how he had mellowed. The brief reformation was hammered together by Geldof whose powers of persuasion had intrigued Nick Mason and finally allowed the tundra-thick ice between Gilmour and Waters to be broken after Waters rang Gilmour. 'Breathe', 'Money', 'Comfortably Numb' and 'Wish You Were Here' tantalized fans worldwide who hoped that Floyd would heed the slogan above the stage 'No More Excuses' and reform.

SEPTEMBER:

Waters' *Ça Ira*

Roger Waters originally began working on what was to become the three-part orchestral opera *Ça Ira* in 1988 when he was inspired by a libretto written by French songwriter Etienne Roda-Gil and his wife Nadine to celebrate the bicentennial anniversary of the French Revolution. Another revolution (the fall of the Berlin Wall) took Waters away from the project, and it was put on hold until 1995. His English-language version with the music for orchestra and choir written in collaboration with Rick Wentworth was finally released in September 2005. Issued on Sony Classical, *Ça Ira* was no mere dabbling with the form but a full-bodied work of maturity that was as compelling and vibrant as the events (the French Revolution not the story of Pink Floyd) that inspired it. Performed in various stages before fully clothed it was presented on a full orchestral catwalk in Rome in November 2005.

NOVEMBER:

UK Music Hall Of Fame

Pink Floyd completed the set when they were inducted into the UK Music Hall of Fame on 16 November 2005. Sadly, on the night of the awards only Nick Mason and David Gilmour were in attendance. Rick Wright was indisposed due to an eye operation and Roger Waters was in Rome working the live staging of his *Ça Ira* opera project, so there was no performance. Gilmour also told the audience that despite their brief Live 8 performance there were no plans for Pink Floyd to reform and tour, although his next solo album was due out in March 2006!

2006

MARCH:

Gilmour's *On An Island*

David Gilmour celebrated his 60th birthday by releasing another solo album *On An Island*. With nothing to prove to anybody he pleased himself with an eclectic wistful bag of songs, mostly co-written with his wife, Polly Samson. These ranged from the solo acoustic murmur of 'Castellorizon' to the compelling harmony dream of the title track that featured David Crosby and Graham Nash sharing vocals and Richard Wright on Hammond organ. The most startling guest was Bob Klose who had been the original Pink Floyd Sound guitarist and had spent the subsequent years making his living as a photographer.

MARCH – AUGUST:

Gilmour's *On An Island* Tour

'I'm rather hoping that with this tour announcement people will believe me when I say, honestly, that this is the only band I plan to tour with,' announced David Gilmour prior to commencing his 2006 promotional tour of *On An Island*. Floyd fans and even Roger Waters, who was making positive noises in the press about reformation, were to be disappointed. As well as his solo material, Gilmour sent sell-out crowds into rapture when revisiting the Floyd back-catalogue. At the Albert Hall encore in London he had a pleased-as-punch David Bowie singing 'Arnold Layne' and 'Comfortably Numb'.

JUNE-MAY 2008:

Waters' *The Dark Side Of The Moon* Tour

Although the Gilmour-led Floyd had performed the entire *Dark Side Of The Moon* material at some venues on their *Division Bell* tour, when Roger Waters announced that he was to tour the album in 2006 there was genuine excitement amongst Floyd fans. *Dark Side* made up the second portion of each show, accompanied by visual effects including a stunning recreation of the rainbow prism of the famed album cover. Whether Waters used vocal backing-tracks and mimed some songs was immaterial as the shows were well received and Nick Mason appeared at some European performances including, predictably, that at the Magny-Cours Formula One race circuit in Nevers, France!

JULY:
Syd Barrett Dies

On the day Roger Waters performed *The Dark Side Of The Moon* in Rotterdam (7 July 2006) Syd Barrett passed away aged 60 in a Cambridge hospital. Like the protagonist in Richard Matheson's classic novel *I Am Legend*, Barrett had become a legend in his own lifetime. That he had moved out of the light due to mental health problems had not dulled the impact of his vital contribution as leader, songwriter and creative force in establishing the foundations upon which Floyd's career was based. Barrett had not died penniless, leaving an estate valued at £1.25 million. The auctioning of personal possessions including jazz CDs, artwork and a self-made bread bin raised over £100,000.

2007
MAY:
Barrett Tribute Concert

The all-star tribute to Syd Barrett held at The Barbican on 10 May 2007 seemed to be a perfect opportunity for Pink Floyd to 'shine on' themselves in tribute to their original leading light. Sadly, although Gilmour, Wright and Mason played the right card in closing the show with 'Arnold Layne', joker in the pack Roger Waters did not join them. Allegedly, he needed to leave before 9 pm to meet his girlfriend! Waters was the only artist to play his own song, 'Flaming Flame', and although he spoke warmly about Barrett, with Richard Wright passing away the following year, the Barbican show was revealed as a perfect reunion opportunity – missed.

JULY: Live Earth

On 7 July 2007, Live Earth: The Concerts For A Climate In Crisis became the largest global entertainment event in history, with simultaneous concerts in New York, London, Sydney, Tokyo, Shanghai, Rio de Janeiro, Johannesburg and Hamburg, reaching an estimated audience of two billion people worldwide. Roger Waters was one of an ear-watering line-up of talent performing at Giants Stadium in New York that included The Police, Alicia Keys and Bon Jovi. Waters delivered a pert seven-song set that included 'Money', 'Us and Them' and 'Another Brick In The Wall (Part 2)'. He was scheduled to appear in the Live Earth concert in Mumbai, India, in December 2008 but this was cancelled due to security fears.

DECEMBER: *Oh, By The Way*

The families of old, young and new Pink Floyd fans had to buy extra-large Christmas stockings in December 2007 when EMI released a retrospective 18-CD box-set of every Pink Floyd album. Although there was no bonus or unreleased material – no *Household Objects* session twangs or *The Big Spliff* ambient tapes from *The Division Bell* sessions – it did showcase the music of one of the most inventive, diverse and commercially successful bands in the world. Each CD was presented as a miniature vinyl replica and fans of Storm Thorgerson (left) could enjoy his latest (and last?) design for the band.

2008

MAY: Gilmour Wins Ivor Novello Award

On 22 May 2008 at the Grosvenor Hotel in London, Dave Gilmour was awarded an 'Ivor': an Ivor Novello Award for his Lifetime Contribution to British music. The award was presented to him by long-time friend and a man who deserved one himself: Robert Wyatt. That the winners were nominated by fellow songwriters made the award a real recognition of Gilmour's talent by peers. On the red carpet prior to the event along with artists like Gabrielle, Mick Hucknall and Gary Barlow from Take That, Gilmour spoke of the importance of the Performing Rights Society who were responsible for collecting royalties from radio stations and other sources every time one of his songs was played.

AUGUS T: **Polar Music Prize**

On 26 August 2008 Roger Waters and Nick Mason travelled to Sweden to receive the Polar Music Prize awarded to Pink Floyd for their exceptional contribution to music. The Polar Prize had been founded by Abba manager and lyricist Stig Anderson in 1989; previous winners include Led Zeppelin, Ray Charles and Paul McCartney. Not only was the award handed out by the King of Sweden, Carl XVI Gustaf, but the band were also awarded one million Swedish Crowns, which worked out at about just over £100,000.

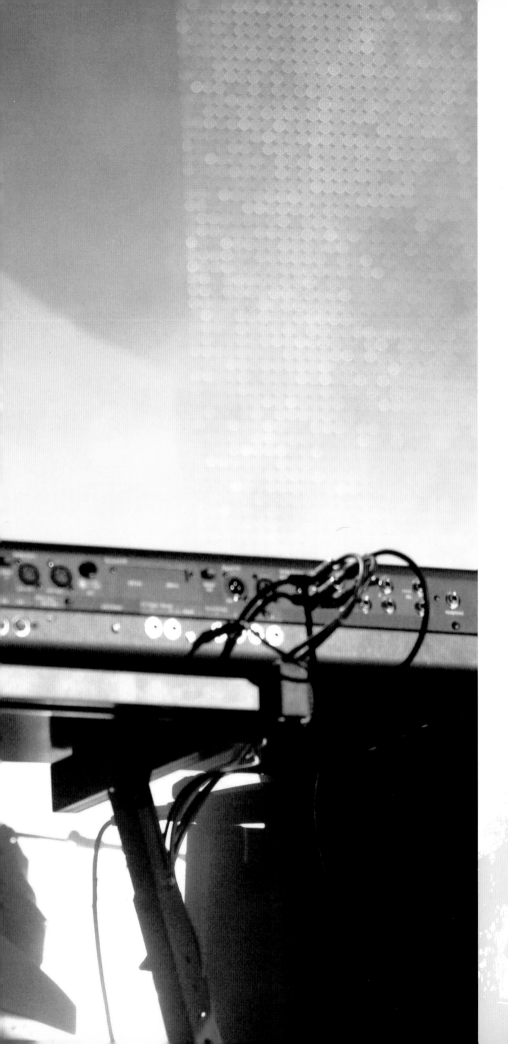

SEPTEMBER: Richard Wright Dies

On 15 September 2008 Richard Wright passed away at his London home aged 65. He had been secretly battling cancer since his diagnosis in December 2007. Obituaries in the media paid full tribute to his trademark organ drones, texture and melodic runs, songwriting and even to early control of the sound effects that panned around auditoriums via early Azimuth co-ordinators. Nick Mason, Roger Waters and Dave Gilmour were united in their emotional statements about their former collaborator and friend. Although quiet and sometimes almost invisible, musically, especially up to 1975, he was the Dark Matter that held the Pink Floyd universe together.

SEPTEMBER:
Gilmour's *Live In Gdansk*

Dave Gilmour's *Live In Gdansk* (2008) had been scheduled for release well before the death of Richard Wright, and its official release a week after Wright's death was a fitting tribute to him. Wright's restrained synth playing in the opening to 'Shine On You Crazy Diamond' is a particular highlight. The album is a live recording of the last concert in Gilmour's *On An Island* tour in 2006 which took place in front of 50,000 in the Gdansk shipyards to celebrate Poland's 1980 revolution. With a 40-piece string orchestra providing backing for some tracks Gilmour was

not only showing solidarity with the Polish movement that began in the shipyards but also with his own and Floyd's compelling back-catalogue.

OCTOBER: Gilmour Wins *Q* Award

David Gilmour received his award for Outstanding Contribution to Music from music magazine *Q* on 6 October 2008 at the Grosvenor Hotel in London's West End. He took the opportunity to pay tribute once again to Richard Wright, saying 'he deserves this just as much as I do. You could say that he worked in the position of second fiddle to the pushier chaps at the front, but his work was vitally important to our entire career.' Gilmour then took a glass and asked the entire audience to stand and toast 'my good friend, Richard Wright'.

INDEX